THE
BEST OF THE
PACIFIC
COOKBOOK

Unique recipes from the Orient, Alaska, Australia,
New Zealand and the islands of the South Pacific

By JACK DENTON SCOTT

A BANTAM PREMIUM BOOK

D1096710

THE BEST OF THE PACIFIC COOKBOOK
A Bantam Premium Book / April 1977

Cover photo Michael Waine

Contents

Foreword

Australia, a continent called a country, named a light, airy dessert Pavlova, to honor the famous dancer when she visited that land down under. Rugged New Zealand pioneers evinced homesickness for England, and their culinary sense of humor, by calling a holiday dish of boned leg of lamb, "Colonial Goose." They discovered "toheroa," a rare and delicious shellfish that tastes like an oyster on a diet of asparagus. In Fiji and Tahiti, they combine the fruits of the sea with the fruit of the coconut palm in such clever ways that this cuisine alone could fill a recipe book.

Japan gives its beef cattle quality beer, daily massages and pampers them in astonishing prima donna style. In Hong Kong they make magic by cooking a suckling pig in a way that makes its crisp skin as delicious as its moist, roasted meat. Hawaii, which that genius with words, Mark Twain, called "the loveliest fleet of islands that lies anchored in any ocean," offers much more than luaus, leis and dancing girls. Hawaiians creatively combine the cuisines of Japan, China, Korea, the Philippines, Puerto Rico, Europe and even America into a cooking style in a class by itself. It is called Hawaiian-Polynesian.

Alaska astounded the rest of the world by making its cold climate produce perhaps the most superb vegetables grown anywhere. Paradoxically, because of very short summers that produce long days of sunshine, plant growth is stimulated, and the cool temperatures so reduce the plants' respiration that they become veritable storehouses of sugar and starch. This gives onions, peas, lettuce, broccoli, potatoes, even rhubarb, flavor and quality found in vegetables no where else on earth. For example, it is not unusual for gardeners in Alaska to grow 70-pound cabbages.

Australia and New Zealand probably lead the world in the production of lamb, mutton and wool. The sheep freely wander the vast lands, herded by natives and sheepmen overseers on horseback. They thrive on the wild grasses and their meat has a flavor unlike lamb elsewhere, slightly gamey—and delectable. With such production, lamb, naturally, holds the place of honor on most menus.

Like Alaska, Australia and New Zealand are rich in fish and game, and in extraordinary vegetables and fruits. Unlike Alaska, they also have excellent beef. There is no such thing as a recipe really indigenous to Australia and New Zealand, unless you consider the bushman's tasteless "damper." Flour and water is mixed until it will hang on a stick, then stuck into a campfire, or a sheepherder's "billy" tea. The latter are tea leaves thrown into a can of boiling water then cooked so long that it is almost strong enough to walk.

But make no mistake, Australians and New Zealanders are much more than poor colonial cousins of Great Britain. They travel a great deal, bring back many ideas, and are inventive, if practical, cooks. They "bake" lettuce and serve a delicate soup made from *kumi kumi*, sort of a wild pumpkin. And where else but Australia and New Zealand would it be considered common practice to cook up a batch of fresh oysters and eggs, and pile them on buttered toast for breakfast?

Australia now is surprising the world and frightening the French with its fine wines. Its Shiraz, Cabernets and Rieslings are so good that they are being clamored for in the export markets.

The islands of the South Pacific, in the Society Islands group, Fiji and Tahiti, despite a French influence, don't do much with wine. However, what they have accomplished with the coconut is astounding. Fiji also learned from its Asian Indian residents how to prepare interesting curries—with, of course, coconut milk. Someone has said that if there were a blight of the coconut palm in the islands, despite the seas teeming with fish, the islanders would probably starve or emigrate, as the Irish did during the potato blight.

A Tahitian saying sums up what the coconut means to the natives: "He who plants a coconut tree not only plants food and drink, dishes and clothing, but a house for himself and a future for his children."

Used in everything from soup to dessert, coconut "milk" has many of the healthful properties of goat's or cow's milk, and its fat is more the equal of butterfat than any other vegetable fat. The Pacific islander also makes his cocktails from the coconut "toddy." He lives in a house of coconut timber roofed with coconut fronds, lights his lamps and cooks with coconut oil, wears some coconut palm clothing and burns coconut husks for fuel.

But it is the milk that he prizes. The milk serves him daily in the preparation of his food in many ways, from poached fish to papaya dessert. That milk is not the liquid found in the coconut when it is split. It is laboriously made from shreds or pieces of the coconut meat, and is somewhat complicated. It can be prepared in five different ways. The most popular method is the mixing of coconut shreds with water, pressing and repressing the liquid and shreds together, then boiling the resultant liquid. The heavier residue that rises to the top is the rich coconut "cream" used in special dishes. The thinner "milk" that remains is used in cooking vegetables and puddings.

But there is more to the menus of the South Pacific islands than the coconut. Their delicate freshwater shrimp, jewel-hued fish, squirrelfish, parrot fish, snapper, rockfish, tuna, even fillets of shark (that taste like swordfish!) are cooked (and uncooked) in many imaginative ways. Fruits, bananas, papayas and pineapples, lemons and limes, the unusual vegetables, taro and breadfruit, and the islands' plump little suckling pigs combine to offer an exotic cuisine, unique in the world. Where else could one get a heavenly dessert of baked puréed fruit called "Poe," an inspired mixture of pineapple, mango, papaya and bananas—and, of course, coconut milk?

Twenty-four hundred miles to the north of the Fiji Islands and Tahiti is Hawaii, the best known islands of Polynesia. It probably has the most confusing cuisine of any civilization. Consistent with her statehood in the U. S., our island state has a "melting pot" menu. Sitting down to dinner in many Hawaiian homes means partaking of the food of about six cultures, ranging from American to Asian. The many peoples lured to this tropical island group, called Hawaii, mainly insisted upon preparing the food they were accustomed to at home. Thus, the present-day confusion. Out of it, as mentioned, came the words that are supposed to explain all, "Hawaiian-Polynesian cooking." And it is certainly interesting.

Few of us, though, could ever get accustomed to a favorite of the Hawaiian old-timers, "poi." Made from taro (a tuber vaguely similar to our potato), poi is literally a mess, a paste made by pounding the peeled, cooked root of the purple taro into a dough. It is then thinned with water into three kinds of poi: one, two and three finger. One-finger poi is thick enough for you to stick a finger into the poi dish, twirl it around and come up with enough to pop into your mouth. The other versions are just thinner poi that require more expertise to get to your mouth. The whole business is self-defeating. The newly-made poi has no flavor at all and looks like wallpaper paste. The aged poi is sourish, somewhat like eating soupy yeast. But wherever you go in Hawaii, there will be poi.

Food on the island of Oahu is, of course, a prime attraction to visitors, but trips to other islands like Maui, Kauai and the Big Island of Hawaii are equally as rewarding, both scenically and gastronomically.

The native island food, however, can be excellent. This includes yams, papaya, coconuts (of course), but mainly pineapple which is shipped all over the world.

The pineapple is to the Hawaiians what the coconut is to the Fijians and Tahitians. Most of us believe that anything "Hawaiian" on a menu means "with pineapple," and it usually does, whether it is authentic Hawaiian or not. Fresh fish is abundant, but not as well prepared or as tasty as in Fiji and Tahiti. Crabs and shellfish are excellent, melons of all kinds are great, and pork is popular. Smoked salmon (Scotch influence), island style, is often served with cocktails.

Most of us, whether we have been to Hawaii or not, know the word "luau," the traditional Hawaiian feast. Created in the old fashioned way, it is an impressive celebration of traditional Hawaiian foods in an atmosphere of music and laughter. In many ways, a luau is somewhat like our New England clam bake, only it is built around roast pig rather than lobsters and clams. The pig is slow-roasted in an underground oven, an "imu," with heated porous stones placed in its cleaned stomach cavity. The pig is then placed into a pit lined with very hot stones, surrounded with yams, breadfruit, and bananas. It is covered with banana, ti, and other tropical leaves, then with earth and steamed a long time. Other typical Hawaiian foods accompany the pig: smoked salmon, chicken laulaus, raw seafood, and, of course, much poi. A good luau is almost impossible to duplicate at home, if you want authentic tropical accompaniments. But some luau food is offered in this book including a pork recipe the author had in the islands. This is an excellent substitute for the whole pig.

Substitutes don't work for the food of Japan and Hong Kong, but luckily, specialty shops make those cuisines possible for American cooks. Several epicures have said, "Japan prepares food for the eye, China for the stomach," as if to say that Japanese food looks good but may not taste as good as it looks, while Chinese food is always a taste sensation. It has also been said that Japan has copied most of her cuisine from China. It is true that Japan has borrowed from the older culture, but she has also added her own creative touches and originated many dishes. And presentation *is* stressed: great attention is paid to using lovely dishes and bowls, always selected for their harmony with the food to be served. But the Japanese do not only intrigue the eye with contrasts in color, textures and shapes, but your taste is pleased simultaneously with foods that are planned to stimulate and capture the appetite.

Four islands, in a chain 1,000 miles long, make up the major portion of Japan. The islands of Kyushu and Shikoku are almost tropical and grow delicate mandarin oranges, lemons, and other citrus fruits. Hokkaido, colder, with weather not unlike New England, is the dairy producer. Temperate Honshu produces the rice and also the people that make Tokyo the largest city in the world.

The waters around Japan are also said to be the world's richest fishing grounds. We have mentioned Japan's famous Kobe beef and its pampered cattle, and will use dishes here inspired by that beef. Japan is also famous for its deep-fried fish and vegetables called *tempura,* and for its national drink *sake,* made by fermenting, then distilling, rice. The world's largest strawberries are grown in Japan, some said to be the size of a clenched fist.

Actually, Japanese food can be outlined in rough categories. *Suimono,* soup; *nimono,* boiled; *yakimono,* broiled; *agemono* or tempura, fried; *mushimono,* steamed; and *nabemono,* open frying pan. Nabemono is usually placed on the table of the diner, and has produced perhaps Japan's most famous dish, *sukiyaki.*

The author of this book doesn't pretend to solve that gastronomical argument about the difference in Japanese and Chinese food, but his own conclusion is that the Japanese are poets of the palate.

Hong Kong came about as the result of a peculiar set of circumstances. After the Opium War (started because of China's displeasure with the British traffic in the drug) the defeated Chinese had to permit free trade at five ports. They had to hand over a twenty-one million dollar indemnity, plus "a properly located island from which Her Majesty's subjects in China may be alike protected and controlled . . ."

Several wars later, over three million Chinese converged on Hong Kong bringing their money and talent to Britain's "properly located island." They converted it into the busiest port in the East, producing and selling nearly everything except airplanes and automobiles. It also is the world's largest shopping center; no taxes or duties on goods make everything a bargain. "China watching" has become one of Hong Kong's more important industries as well. Journalists and businessmen maintain contact with the People's Republic from the British colony leased from China for 99 years in 1898.

The Chinese refugees that poured into Hong Kong brought cooking techniques from Canton, Peking, Shanghai, Szechuan, Foochow and Swatow, making the island probably the one place in the world where all of the superb cuisine of China is well represented.

Today, because of this, Hong Kong rhymes with heaven with many Chinese, exemplifying their ancient proverb, "Food is the heaven of the ordinary people."

From the fragrant harbor of Hong Kong to Alaska's snowy peaks, from Tahiti's palmy beaches and Australia and New Zealand's vast lands down under to teeming Tokyo, the peoples of the Pacific have a common denominator: an original, imaginative touch with food that pleases all of our palates—and always offers surprises.

Here, in a modest, yet selective book, are the recipes of some of the best of those surprising and delicious dishes. The recipes range from the magical way of "cooking" a fish with fresh lime juice (without heat) to stuffing a steak with oysters. Enjoy!

J. D. S.

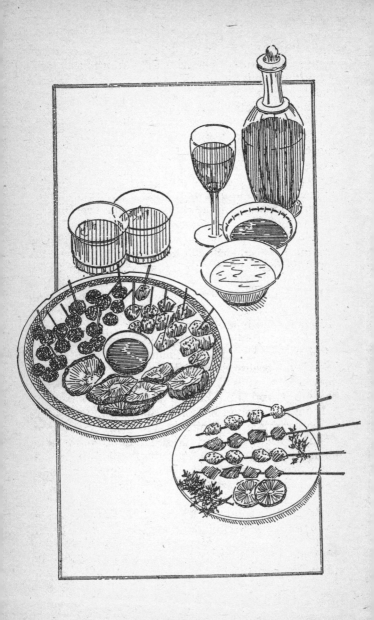

1
Appetizers

Converting a chicken gizzard into a delicacy; making the common potato a conversation-stopper; shaving the meat of the coconut wafer-thin and baking it into a delicious morsel that makes people forget their cocktail and reach for more; melding little pieces of chicken, pork, beef or fish in mysterious Oriental spices then broiling them and offering them with drinks as "*satés*;" blending fish with egg into a delectable "fish roll;" these are just a few Pacific touches with appetizers. It's enough to make a person go on the drinking-man's diet and forget all about dinner.

FIJI BREADFRUIT CHIPS

MAKES ABOUT 80 CHIPS:

1 half-ripe breadfruit	½ cup of salt
2 quarts of water	3 cups of cooking oil

Peel, core and cut the breadfruit into quarters, then cut lengthwise into paper-thin slices. Add the ½ cup of salt to the water and soak the breadfruit slices for 2 hours. Drain and dry well with paper towels. In a pot, wok or deep-fryer heat the oil, but not until smoking. Cook the breadfruit slices until crisply golden. Drain well. Sprinkle lightly with salt and serve them when they are cool enough to handle but still hot.

STEAMED ALASKAN KING CRAB

SERVES 6 TO 8:

This simple Alaskan favorite may be the best way to serve their prized seafood.

2 tablespoons of olive oil	4 pounds of Alaska king
3 cloves of garlic	crab legs, in their shell
10 cracked peppercorns	½ pound of butter,
2 small bay leaves	melted

In a deep pot, in 2 cups of boiling water, place the oil, garlic, peppercorns and bay leaves. On a steaming platform, well above the water, place the crab legs, cover the pot and steam for 25 minutes. Strain the melted butter through cheesecloth to remove the white sediment, and pour, very hot, into six bowls. Diners will crack the shells and dip the succulent white meat into the butter.

HAWAIIAN CHICKEN LAULAUS

SERVES 8:

1 pound of salt pork, diced

2 pounds of boned chicken breasts, cut into ½-inch cubes

3 pounds of taro leaves, Swiss chard or Chinese *bok choy*, cleaned and cut into ¼-inch-wide strips, 1 inch long

10 scallions, minced

24 ti leaves, or the husks from 8 ears of corn

8 sheets of aluminum foil cut 8 x 14 inches

The fillings vary with mixtures of pork, fish and chicken and make delightful appetizers, with each guest unfolding his own laulau.

In a saucepan, sauté the salt pork until crisp. Stir in the chicken and cook for 5 minutes. Add the taro or chard or *bok choy* strips and cook for 4 minutes. Stir in the scallions, blending well. Lay out the sheets of foil, center each with the ti leaves or cornhusks, with the leaves overlapping at the center. Place a generous amount of the chicken mixture (dividing it equally) in the center of each arrangement of ti leaves. Pull the corners of the foil together, twist them tightly to form a neat, tight bundle. Place them on a rack in a large pot and pour boiling water around them to a depth of 1 inch. Cover the pot and simmer for 40 minutes.

CHICKEN TERIYAKI WITH
SESAME SEEDS
(Japan)

SERVES 6 TO 8:

2 pounds of boned chicken thighs, cut into ½-inch pieces

10 tablespoons of soy sauce

7 tablespoons of sake or dry white wine

8 tablespoons of sesame seed oil

2 cloves of garlic, crushed

4 teaspoons of fresh minced ginger

10 tablespoons of sesame seeds, pan toasted

In a bowl, blend the chicken, soy sauce, sake (or wine), oil, garlic and ginger. Marinate for four hours, turning several times. Drain and skewer the chicken on bamboo picks or shish kebab skewers. Broil for 3 minutes, turn and broil for another 3 minutes. Roll in the toasted sesame seeds and serve on the skewers.

HAWAIIAN COCONUT CHIPS

MAKES 3 CUPS:

1 fresh coconut, about 2 pounds, shelled and peeled	¾ teaspoon of salt

Cut the coconut meat into 2-inch-long, wafer-thin slices. Evenly spread them in one layer on a shallow baking pan or cookie sheet. Sprinkle them with salt and bake in a preheated 325-degree oven for 25 minutes, stirring from time to time, until evenly browned and crisp. Cool before serving.

EGG AND FISH ROLL ZENSAI

(Japan)

SERVES 6:

½ pound of fillets of a white-fleshed fish such as halibut or sole, finely chopped	4 tablespoons of dry sherry
	2 tablespoons of water
	2 tablespoons of sugar
8 eggs, beaten	½ teaspoon of salt
4 tablespoons of soy sauce	3 tablespoons of peanut oil

In a bowl, blend all ingredients except the oil. Heat 1 tablespoon of oil in a 6 x 6 square pan. Pour in one-third of the egg-fish mixture. Cook over medium heat for 4 minutes, carefully turn and cook 2 minutes longer, or until set. Remove, roll, while hot, in jelly roll fashion. Cool, seam side down. Repeat the cooking and rolling procedure until the mixture is used. Cool the rolls for 40 minutes, then cut them into ½-inch-thick slices and serve with bowls of soy sauce in which the slices can be dipped.

FIJI PICKLED FISH

SERVES 4:

2 pounds of cod or
mackerel fillets, cut
into bite-sized pieces
1½ teaspoons of salt
1 cup of flour
3 tablespoons of cooking
oil

4 medium-sized onions,
coarsely chopped
1 cup of white vinegar
1 tablespoon of curry
powder
1 tablespoon of
cornstarch

Season the fish with salt and dredge with flour
(shaking off any excess). In a saucepan, heat the oil
and evenly brown the fish. Cook the onions in a small
amount of boiling water until they are soft. Drain and
return the onions to the pot. Add the vinegar and
bring to a boil. Blend the curry powder with the cornstarch and stir into the onion-vinegar pot, simmering
until thickened. In a deep serving dish, alternate
layers of fish with the onion mixture and serve cold.

FIJI FISH APPETIZER

SERVES 8:

4 cups of raw mackerel
fillets, cut into bite-
sized pieces
1½ teaspoons of salt
1½ cups of fresh lemon
juice

2 small carrots, scraped
and grated
4 scallions, chopped
1 cup of Thick Fiji Coco-
nut Cream (see below)

In a bowl, place the fish pieces, add the salt and
lemon juice and gently mix. Cover and refrigerate for
2 hours, gently mixing once or twice during that
period. Drain the fish. In another bowl, place the
drained fish, carrots and scallions and the Thick Fiji

Coconut Cream. Toss gently and refrigerate for 1 hour.
Serve cold as a first course or an appetizer.

THICK FIJI COCONUT CREAM

Place the meat from 2 medium-sized coconuts, cut
into small pieces, into an electric blender. Turn on
high until grated, turning machine off from time to
time to stir up contents. Place this grated coconut in
cheesecloth and, over a bowl, squeeze tightly. The
liquid is the coconut cream. Meat of half a coconut
should produce ¼ cup of cream.

LAMB TIDBITS
(Australia and New Zealand)

SERVES 6:

*Australians and New Zealanders aren't big on appe-
tizers, but they do like this one taught them by Greek
immigrants who continue to arrive in both countries.
As lamb is also a favorite of the Greeks, this was a
natural for all residents. Some say the Greeks are
drawn to Australia and New Zealand because of the
high quality and low price of the lamb.*

2 pounds of lean lamb from the leg, cut into ½-inch cubes	1 teaspoon of pepper
	Juice of 3 lemons mixed with 2 teaspoons of dry oregano
2 teaspoons of salt	

Place the lamb in equal portions on 6 skewers.
Sprinkle evenly with salt and pepper. Cook, preferably
over charcoal or under a broiler, about 8 minutes,
turning constantly so the meat browns evenly. Be
careful not to overcook; the meat should be moist and
pink inside. Pour the lemon juice mixture into a wide
flat plate. Roll the lamb cubes on the skewers in it,
coating well, then broil again 20 seconds on each side.
Serve on the skewers.

LOMI LOMI LIVERS
(Hawaii)

SERVES 6 TO 8:

1 pound of chicken livers, cut into bite-sized pieces

4 tablespoons of Hoisin Sauce (available in specialty shops)

Batter (see below)

3 cups of cooking oil

In a bowl mix the livers with the Hoisin Sauce, tossing gently to coat the livers well. Marinate for 4 hours. Spoon the livers into the batter and deep-fry in hot but not smoking oil in a pot, wok or deep-fryer, a few at a time. Don't crowd them in the fryer. Cook each batch 1½ minutes, or until crisply brown outside and pink inside. Overcooking can make them tasteless, with the batter having the predominant personality.

BATTER

1½ cups of flour

3 tablespoons of cornstarch

2 teaspoons of salt

2 teaspoons of baking powder

1 cup of water

Place all of the ingredients in a bowl and blend well.

MOTSU
(Japan)

SERVES 8:

In the form of tasty appetizers, the Japanese have a unique way of serving chicken gizzards, a part of the bird that too many of us waste. The gizzards can *simply be cut in two and served, but the Japanese trim them so they look like little meatballs.*

2 pounds of chicken gizzards	6 cloves of garlic, crushed
2 cups of soy sauce	2 tablespoons of minced fresh ginger root
1 cup of sugar	2 cups of water

Place all ingredients in a pot, bring to a boil, cover, lower heat and simmer for 1 hour, or until the gizzards are tender. Serve on small bamboo picks or toothpicks, either hot or cold, with a dip of soy sauce, or *wasabi*, Japanese horseradish.

GINGER PORK BALLS
(*Hong Kong*)

SERVES 6 TO 8:

1½ pounds of ground lean pork	1 teaspoon of salt
1 egg, beaten	1½ tablespoons of grated fresh ginger root
½ cup of minced water chestnuts	½ cup of bread crumbs
1½ tablespoons of soy sauce	Peanut oil

In a bowl, blend well the pork, egg, water chestnuts, soy sauce, salt, ginger and bread crumbs. Form into small, compact balls. In a wok or deep-fryer, heat the oil and cook the pork balls until browned. Serve warm on toothpicks with a dipping sauce of your choice.

HONG KONG BLACK MUSHROOMS

SERVES 6 TO 8:

12 ounces of dry black
Oriental mushrooms
6 cups of chicken broth
⅓ cup of peanut oil

6 tablespoons of soy
sauce
2 teaspoons of sugar
½ teaspoon of sesame
seed oil

Place the mushrooms in a bowl and cover with boiling water. Let stand for 30 minutes, drain well, then discard stems. In a casserole or baking dish, place the whole mushrooms, add the chicken broth, cover the dish and cook in a preheated 250-degree oven for 2 hours. In a deep saucepan, heat the peanut oil, add the mushrooms and chicken broth, stir in the soy sauce and sugar and simmer for 5 minutes. Chill; just before serving, stir in the sesame seed oil.

FRIED YASAWA PORK BALLS

(*Hawaii*)

SERVES 6 TO 8:

3 cups of cooked, minced lean pork

2½ cups of bread crumbs

2 large eggs, beaten separately

1 tablespoon of minced parsley

1 teaspoon of salt

½ teaspoon of pepper

2 cups of cooking oil

In a bowl, blend well the pork, 1 cup of the bread crumbs, 1 beaten egg, the parsley, salt and pepper. Form into small balls, dip into the remaining beaten egg, then roll in the remaining bread crumbs. In a pot, wok or deep-fryer, heat the oil until hot but not smoking and cook the pork balls until crisply brown. Watch carefully, they can overcook easily. Serve warm or cold with a dip of your choice.

ISLAND ROAST PORK
(*Hawaii*)

SERVES 8 TO 10:

This is a versatile roasting of pork which can be passed with cocktails, or used as a tasty base for a dinner, stir-frying it with a variety of vegetables and a dash of soy sauce. The blending with snow peas, bean sprouts, mushrooms, water chestnuts, etc. can lift the simple slices of meat into another category, and slicing the pork very thin and mixing it with fried rice gives it yet another personality.

1 cup of chicken broth
½ teaspoon of Five Chinese Spices Powder (available in specialty shops)
3 tablespoons of sake or dry sherry
1 tablespoon of soy sauce
4 tablespoons of red bean curd (available in specialty shops)

½ cup of dark brown sugar
2 teaspoons of salt
⅓ cup of Hoisin Sauce (available in specialty shops)
1 (5-pound) pork butt, boned and most of the fat removed, cut into strips 1 inch thick, 3 inches long, 2 inches wide

In a bowl combine and blend well all the ingredients except the pork. Now add the pork and toss well, blending it with the sauce. Cover the bowl and marinate for 8 hours. Reserve the marinade for basting. Arrange the pork on a rack in a roasting pan well above 2 inches of hot water. Roast, uncovered, in a preheated 350-degree oven for 30 minutes. Turn the pork over, baste well and roast for 30 minutes longer, or until tender. Cut the pork into ¼-inch-thick slices and pass hot or cold as appetizers.

POTATO ZENSAI
(Japan)

SERVES 6:

Japanese hors d'oeuvres, called zensai, *can range from elaborate to the simple.*

3 (7-ounce) potatoes (preferably Idaho "bakers") boiled in their jackets until cooked but still quite firm

3 small eggs, beaten
2 cups of bread crumbs
Oil for deep-frying
Bowls of soy sauce

Peel the potatoes and cut into 1-inch cubes. Carefully thread them on skewers or bamboo picks, dip in the beaten egg, then roll in the bread crumbs and deep fry. Drain and serve with soy sauce.

SOUTH PACIFIC SATÉ
(Fiji and Tahiti)

SERVES 6 TO 8:

This recipe can be varied, using chicken, pork, beef, even ground fish. Chicken is popular.

4 cloves of garlic, minced ⎫
1 teaspoon of salt   ⎬ blended into a paste
½ teaspoon of pepper   ⎭

½ teaspoon of ground coriander

2 tablespoons of dark brown sugar

3 tablespoons of soy sauce

4 tablespoons of fresh lime juice

3 whole chicken breasts, skinned, boned and cut into 1-inch pieces

In a large bowl, place garlic paste, coriander, sugar, soy sauce and lime juice, blending well. Add the chicken pieces, toss gently to coat evenly and marinate in the refrigerator for 4 hours, turning once or twice during this time. Let chicken set until it is at room temperature, then thread on skewers and broil for 5 minutes, turning often, until chicken is crisply browned.

CHINESE SPARERIBS
(Hong Kong)

SERVES 8:

½ cup of dry sherry

¾ cup of soy sauce

2 cloves of garlic, mashed

½ teaspoon of ground cinnamon

½ cup of dark brown sugar

½ teaspoon of ground ginger

¼ teaspoon of black pepper

5 pounds of spareribs, cut into single ribs, with excess fat removed

In a bowl, blend well all ingredients except the spareribs. Place the ribs in a flat dish, cover with the marinade and let stand for 4 hours, occasionally turning the ribs to coat them. Drain the ribs, place on a broiler rack over a pan and broil, turning and basting often for 35 minutes, or until the spareribs are crisp and evenly browned.

2
Soups

Blend a dash of Oriental cunning with a soup-spoon of Alaskan simplicity, add a touch of Australian and New Zealand originality with a spicing of Hawaiian daring, and you come up with a soup chapter without equal.

The people of the Pacific, dressing their soups with everything from avocados and lotus roots to pumpkins and peanuts, perhaps have the most unusual first-course offering in the world.

AVOCADO SOUP

(*Tahiti*)

SERVES 4:

2 tablespoons of butter
1 tablespoon of flour
1 cup of milk
4 cups of chicken broth

2 small, very ripe avocados, peeled and mashed
1 teaspoon of salt
½ teaspoon of pepper

In a pot, over low heat, melt the butter and stir in the flour, stirring into a smooth golden paste. Gradually stir in the milk, simmering and stirring until smooth and somewhat thickened. Stir in the chicken broth and bring to a simmer, stirring. Stir in the avocados, salt and pepper and bring to a simmer. Do not boil. Taste for seasoning.

ALASKAN CABBAGE SOUP

SERVES 6:

This soup was adapted, or copied, by the Alaskans from the Russian "Shchee," a reminder that the Russians once wandered and almost owned Alaska.

3 tablespoons of butter
1 small turnip, scraped and coarsely chopped
2 medium-sized onions, coarsely chopped
4 small carrots, scraped and coarsely chopped
1 quart of rich caribou or moose (or beef) stock
1 teaspoon of salt
½ teaspoon of pepper
2 small bay leaves
1 tablespoon of fresh chopped dill, or 1 teaspoon of dried dillweed
6 small potatoes, peeled and quartered
1 (3-pound) firm head of cabbage, cut into wedges and cored, with tough ribs removed

In a saucepan, melt the butter and sauté the turnip, onion and carrots for 10 minutes. In a large pot, pour the stock, bring to a boil, reduce to a simmer and stir in the turnip, onion, carrots, salt, pepper, bay leaves and dill. Cover and cook for 25 minutes. Add the potatoes, cover and simmer for 15 minutes, or until the potatoes can barely be pierced with a fork. Increase the heat to medium, remove pot cover, and add the cabbage wedges, pushing down into the stock. Alaskans then only cook the cabbage for 5 minutes, but if you want it less crunchy, increase the cooking time to your taste. Taste for seasoning. Remove the bay leaves. The Russians added a big spoonful of sour cream to their soup bowls. Alaskans don't bother.

CRAB SOUP QUEENSLAND STYLE

(*Australia*)

SERVES 6:

4 tablespoons of butter
2 medium-sized onions, chopped
2 medium-sized stalks of celery, chopped
4 tablespoons of flour
1 quart of milk
Pinch of cayenne
1½ teaspoons of salt

1 pound of cooked fresh or frozen crabmeat (shell and cartilage removed), cut into small pieces
1 cup of heavy cream
2 tablespoons of sherry
2 teaspoons of fresh lemon juice
2 tablespoons of finely chopped parsley

In a soup pot, over medium heat, melt the butter and cook the onion and celery until soft. Blend the flour in well. Lower heat and gradually pour in the milk, stirring constantly. Add the cayenne and salt, and cook, uncovered, stirring occasionally, until the soup is smooth and the consistency of heavy cream. Remove from the heat and strain. Return the liquid to the pot, stir in the crabmeat and the cream; bring to a simmer. Blend in the sherry and lemon juice and serve immediately with parsley sprinkled atop.

HONG KONG CRAB SOUP

SERVES 6:

4 tablespoons of peanut oil	½ teaspoon of salt
2 slices of fresh ginger root	2 tablespoons of dry sherry
3 whole scallions, finely chopped	6 cups of chicken broth
1 cup of crabmeat, flaked	2 egg whites, stiffly beaten
2 tablespoons of chicken broth ⎫ blended	4 tablespoons of medium cream
2 teaspoons of cornstarch ⎭	

In a saucepan, heat the oil and sauté the ginger and scallions for 2 minutes. Blend in the crabmeat, salt and sherry, and cook, stirring, for 1 minute. Pour in the chicken broth and bring to a boil, discarding the ginger. Turn heat to low. Blend the egg whites with the cream and the chicken broth-cornstarch mixture and stir it into the crab soup. Simmer, stirring, for 2 minutes.

LOTUS ROOT SOUP

(*Hong Kong*)

SERVES 8:

4 segments of lotus root (lotus roots, resembling reddish-brown sausages, are available in specialty shops)

1½ pounds of lean pork, sliced wafer thin

2 teaspoons of cornstarch

2 tablespoons of soy sauce

8 cups of chicken broth

½ teaspoon of salt

½ teaspoon of pepper

Scrape and wash well the lotus root segments, cutting off and discarding the ends of each joint. Cut into halves, lengthwise, then crosswise into ½-inch-thick pieces. Blend the pork slices with the cornstarch and soy sauce. In a pot, bring the chicken broth to a boil. Add the salt and pepper. Stir in the pork mixture and the lotus root, cover the pot and simmer for 45 minutes, or until the lotus root is tender and the pork cooked through. Taste for seasoning.

MISOTAKI SOUP

(As served in Hawaii by the Japanese)

SERVES 6 TO 8:

1½ cups of dried pea beans

2½ teaspoons of salt

3 tablespoons of white vinegar

2 tablespoons of light soy sauce

8 cups of chicken broth

4 small carrots, scraped and thinly sliced

4 small white onions, thinly sliced

1½ pounds of pork loin, cut into very thin strips

½ teaspoon of pepper

1 cup of cellophane noodles, blanched

6 scallions, with tops, minced

Pick over the beans, discarding discolored and broken ones, then rinse well in cold water. In a pot, place 1 quart of hot water, 1 teaspoon of the salt, the beans, and bring to a boil. Cover and soak for 1 hour. Drain. Place in a pot with fresh water, cover and simmer for 1 hour, or until very tender. Drain and mash the beans. Place them in a bowl, blend in the vinegar and soy sauce; cover and refrigerate overnight. In a pot, bring the chicken broth to a boil, stir in the carrots, onion, pork, remaining 1½ teaspoons salt and pepper. Stir in the mashed beans and cook for 35 minutes, or until the vegetables and pork are just tender. Stir in the noodles. Taste for seasoning. Serve very hot in bowls garnished with the scallions.

NIKU DANGO SUIMONO
(Japanese Meatball Soup)

SERVES 8:

½ pound of ground beef
½ pound of ground lean pork
1 tablespoon of minced fresh ginger root
3 eggs, slightly beaten
2 tablespoons of flour
2 teaspoons of soy sauce
½ teaspoon of salt

10 cups of chicken broth
8 small carrots, parboiled whole, then cut diagonally into ¼-inch slices
4 ounces of vermicelli, cooked, drained and kept hot
8 sprigs of watercress

In a bowl, blend well the beef, pork, ginger, eggs, flour, soy sauce and salt. Make tiny meatballs. In a pot, bring the chicken broth to a boil, add the carrots, reduce heat to simmer, then add the meatballs. As the meatballs are soft and may break up if just dropped in, gently lower them on a slotted spoon. Cook for 15 minutes. Place the vermicelli in 8 soup bowls, fill with broth and meatballs and garnish with watercress.

PORK AND WATERCRESS SOUP
(Hong Kong)

SERVES 6:

1 pound of lean pork
1 teaspoon of salt
½ teaspoon of pepper
1½ tablespoons of cornstarch

8 cups of chicken broth
3 bunches of watercress

Slice the pork into shreds. The Chinese often freeze the pork until it is very firm, but not solidly frozen, making it easier to slice in any form. Sprinkle the pork shreds with salt, pepper and cornstarch. Bring 2 cups of the chicken broth to a boil, add the pork and simmer for 4 minutes. Remove the pork with a slotted spoon. In another pot, bring the remaining 6 cups of chicken broth to a boil, add the pork and simmer for 10 minutes. Stir in the watercress; simmer for 3 minutes, separating the sprigs as it cooks. Taste and adjust the seasoning. In Hong Kong, this is served in a large tureen with a ladle for guests to fill their own soup bowls.

NEW ZEALAND PUMPKIN AND CHEESE SOUP

SERVES 8:

7 cups of chicken broth
3 cups of peeled, sliced, uncooked pumpkin
¾ cup of lentils, rinsed, soaked 3 hours and drained

1½ teaspoons of salt
½ teaspoon of pepper
3 tablespoons of grated sharp Cheddar cheese

In a pot, bring the broth to a boil, add the pumpkin and lentils, reduce to a simmer, season with salt and pepper, cover and cook for 1 hour, or until the lentils are soft. Remove the pumpkin and lentils, place them in a strainer and force through the strainer back into the broth in the soup pot. Taste for seasoning. Stir in the cheese, bring to a simmer and serve immediately.

PEANUT SOUP

(Fiji)

SERVES 8:

6 cups of milk
1 teaspoon of salt
½ teaspoon of pepper
3 cups of minced, freshly
    roasted peanuts

2 tablespoons of butter
2 tablespoons of finely
    grated carrot
2 tablespoons of finely
    chopped parsley

In a pot, place the milk, salt, pepper and the peanuts and blend well. Bring to a boil, lower heat and simmer for 10 minutes. Just before serving stir in the butter. Taste for seasoning. Garnish each bowl with the carrot and parsley.

TART RHUBARB SOUP

(Alaska)

SERVES 6 TO 8:

1 quart of chicken broth
¾ pound of chicken
    livers, quartered
4 cups of rhubarb,
    trimmed and cut into
    1-inch pieces

4 small whole cloves
    Juice of 1 lemon
1½ teaspoons of salt
½ teaspoon of pepper

In a heavy pot, pour in the chicken broth and bring to a boil. Stir in the chicken livers, rhubarb, cloves, lemon juice, salt and pepper. Cover and simmer for 10 minutes, or until the livers are firm but not hard and the rhubarb is tender. Remove the cloves before serving.

SCALLOP STEW

(Alaska)

SERVES 6 TO 8:

Only Alaskans are so rich in scallops that they can stew them. But it is worth it, even if you have to buy the scallops many miles from the source, as the flavor is delicate and unique.

5 tablespoons of butter	1 teaspoon of salt
4 cups of bay scallops, left whole, or sea scallops, halved	½ teaspoon of pepper
	1 tablespoon of chopped parsley
6 cups of medium cream	

In a pot, melt 3 tablespoons of the butter and sauté the scallops for 3 minutes. Stir in the cream, salt and pepper, bring to a boil, reduce to a bare simmer and cook, stirring occasionally, for 10 minutes, or until the scallops are firm but tender (do not overcook as they will toughen). Just before serving stir in the remaining 2 tablespoons of butter and serve sprinkled with the parsley.

TASMANIAN SCALLOP SOUP

(Australia)

SERVES 6:

4 tablespoons of butter	1½ teaspoons of salt
4 tablespoons of flour	½ teaspoon of pepper
4 cups of milk	⅛ teaspoon of mace
1 teaspoon of anchovy paste	1 pound of Tasmanian scallops, chopped
1 teaspoon of fresh lemon juice	2 tablespoons of chopped parsley

In a large saucepan, melt the butter, stir in the flour, cooking over low heat until the paste is smooth and golden. Gradually stir in the milk, cooking and stirring over low heat, until smooth and the consistency of heavy cream. Stir in the anchovy paste, lemon juice, salt, pepper and mace. Bring to a simmer, stir in the scallops and simmer for 10 minutes. Scallops should be firm but tender (do not overcook or they'll toughen). Serve with parsley sprinkled atop.

TARO AND BREADFRUIT SOUP

(Tahiti)

SERVES 8 TO 10:

2 tablespoons of peanut oil

½ pound of lean pork, cut into ½-inch cubes

1 pound of taros (a nutty-flavored island vegetable that looks like a small, warty potato with bluish-gray flesh), peeled and cubed

1 small breadfruit, peeled and cubed

4 small carrots, scraped and coarsely chopped

2 medium-sized onions, coarsely chopped

1 medium-sized, half-ripe papaya, peeled and coarsely chopped

3 medium-sized ripe tomatoes, peeled and coarsely chopped

2 small bay leaves

⅛ teaspoon of ground turmeric

1½ teaspoons of salt

1 teaspoon of pepper

2 quarts of chicken broth

In a large pot, heat the oil and cook the pork over medium heat, turning often, for 10 minutes, or until evenly browned. Add the taro, breadfruit, carrots, onion, papaya, tomatoes, bay leaves, turmeric, salt and pepper. Pour in the chicken broth, cover, bring to a boil, then lower the heat and cook, covered, for 45 minutes, or until the pork is tender. Taste for seasoning. Remove the pork and bay leaves and place soup in an electric blender on high for 30 seconds. Serve in hot bowls with the pork cubes evenly distributed.

TOHEROA SOUP

(*New Zealand*)

SERVES 6:

12 *toheroa* (large shellfish similar to clams) or clams	6 cups of milk
	2 teaspoons of curry powder
6 tablespoons of butter	1½ teaspoons of salt
4 tablespoons of flour	½ teaspoon of pepper

Remove the *toheroa* (or clams) from their shells, reserving the liquor, and mince. In a saucepan over medium heat, melt the butter and add the flour, stirring into a smooth paste. Gradually stir in the *toheroa* liquor, then the milk, stirring until slightly thickened and smooth. Add the minced shellfish, curry, salt and pepper, blend well and simmer for 10 minutes. The *toheroa* (or clams) shouldn't be overcooked.

TOMATO-RICE SOUP

(*Fiji*)

SERVES 4:

4 cups of water	1 small red pepper, seeded, cored and thinly sliced
1 cup of rice	
2 tablespoons of butter	
2 small onions, chopped	1 teaspoon of salt
2 medium-sized tomatoes, peeled and chopped	1 teaspoon of sugar

In a pot, bring the water to a boil. Stir in the rice and simmer for 30 minutes. In a saucepan, melt the butter and sauté the onion until soft. Add the tomatoes and pepper and cook for 10 minutes. Rub this mixture through a strainer into the rice pot, stir in the salt and sugar. Taste for seasoning.

MISO VEGETABLE NOODLE SOUP

(*Japan*)

SERVES. 4:

5 cups of chicken broth

½ pound of lean pork, cut into ½-inch cubes

1 large onion, chopped

¼ cup of fresh cleaned shrimp, cut into ¼-inch pieces

1 cup of shredded white turnip

2 cups of cooked *udon* (narrow egg noodles)

½ teaspoon of salt

¼ teaspoon of pepper

6 tablespoons of *miso* (white soybean paste)

In a pot, bring broth to a boil, add the pork and onion. Lower heat and simmer for 20 minutes, or until the pork is tender. Stir in the shrimp, turnip, *udon*, salt and pepper, and simmer, stirring gently, for 5 minutes. In a small bowl, place the soybean paste and mix it well with 6 spoonfuls of stock from the pot. Stir it into the pot, bring to a boil and serve immediately.

3
Fish and Shellfish

When it comes to fish and shellfish cookery, no one anywhere can rival the reputation of those islands and lands that rim the vast Pacific. From the cold-water species off Alaska, to the warm sea varieties that are the specialties of Fiji and Tahiti, come enough creative combinations of recipes to fill a book.

From peppered shrimp to brandied crab, from simple bagged salmon to potted oysters, there is enough variety to tempt any appetite, and evidence of such richness of resource to stir envy in all of us who are not Pacific residents.

COD SOUTH SEA ISLAND STYLE

(*Fiji*)

SERVES 8:

2 (2-pound) cod fillets,
   ¾ inch thick, cut into 8
   equal pieces
⅓ cup of fresh lime juice
1 teaspoon of salt
½ teaspoon of pepper
¼ teaspoon of marjoram

⅓ cup of melted butter
½ pound of shrimp, in
   their shells
½ cup of sour cream
6 scallions, with tops,
   thinly sliced

In a shallow baking dish, place the fish and pour the lime juice over it. Let set for 10 minutes, turn the fish, spoon the juice over it, let set again for 10 minutes. Pour off the lime juice. Season the fish with salt and pepper and the marjoram and pour the melted butter over it. Broil for 10 minutes, basting twice with the buttery pan juices. Set the fish aside to cool slightly. Cook the shrimp for 5 minutes in enough boiling water to cover them. Remove shrimp (reserve the water), cool enough to handle and shell. Return the shells to the pot of water in which the shrimp were cooked. On high heat, boil the shrimp shells until the water is reduced by two-thirds. Blend 2 teaspoons of the shrimp water with the sour cream and spoon over the cod in the baking dish. Bake, uncovered, in a preheated 325-degree oven for 30 minutes, or until the fish flakes easily when tested with a fork. Garnish with the shrimps (warmed) and the sliced scallions.

ALASKAN CRAB OMELET

SERVES 6:

6 large eggs
6 tablespoons of light
    cream
1 teaspoon of salt
½ teaspoon of pepper

1 pound of snow crab-
    meat, coarsely chopped
3 tablespoons of butter
1 onion, finely chopped

In a bowl, combine and beat well the eggs, cream, salt and pepper. Blend in the crabmeat. In a large frypan, melt the butter and sauté the onion until soft. Pour into the frypan the egg-crabmeat mixture and cook for about 4 minutes, or until the bottom is set and golden. To turn, place a plate, inverted, on top of the frypan, flip the omelet onto the plate, cooked side up, then slide the omelet back into the frypan. Cook for another 4 minutes, or until golden on the outside but moist and soft inside. This is more of an Italian *frittata* than a conventional omelet, which is folded.

BRANDIED KING CRAB

(*Alaska*)

SERVES 6:

2 pounds of king crab leg
    meat
½ cup of flour

½ cup of butter
4 ounces of brandy
Juice of 1 lemon

Dredge the meat lightly in flour. In a saucepan, melt the butter over high heat and sauté the crabmeat quickly, turning until it is an even golden brown. Pour in the brandy and lemon juice, stir well and cook for 3 minutes. Do not overcook.

KING CRAB CASSEROLE
(*Alaska*)

SERVES 4:

Alaskans are purists with their king crab (like the fishermen in Iran who eat caviar with a spoon and disdain the fancy fixings of lemon and chopped egg), mainly steaming it, cracking the shells and dipping the meat in melted butter. But on occasion when they have guests and some wild mushrooms on hand they'll whip up this dish.

3 tablespoons of butter
1 cup of chopped fresh
  mushrooms
1 tablespoon of flour
½ cup of heavy cream
1 pound of king crab
  meat, cut into bite-sized
  pieces
Juice of ½ lemon

1 teaspoon of capers,
  rinsed and drained
1 teaspoon of chopped
  parsley
2 egg whites, beaten stiff

In a saucepan, melt 2 tablespoons of the butter and sauté the mushrooms for 2 minutes. Stir in the flour, blend, cook 2 minutes, add the cream and cook 2 minutes. Stir in the crabmeat, lemon juice, capers, parsley and egg whites. With the remaining 1 tablespoon butter, butter a casserole and pour in the mixture. Cook, uncovered, in a preheated 350-degree oven for 15 minutes, or until brown and bubbling.

SNOW CRAB CAKES

(Alaska)

SERVES 6 TO 8:

2 pounds of snow crab meat
½ teaspoon of Coleman's dry mustard
4 tablespoons of mayonnaise
2 small eggs, beaten

1 teaspoon of salt
½ teaspoon of pepper
⅛ teaspoon of cayenne
2 cups of bread crumbs
5 tablespoons of butter
1 tablespoon of cooking oil

In a bowl blend well the crabmeat, mustard, mayonnaise, eggs, salt, pepper, cayenne and ½ cup of the bread crumbs. When well mixed, form into cakes. Dredge with remaining bread crumbs. In a large frypan, heat the butter and oil and brown the cakes evenly. Drain on paper towels.

TOMATO-BAKED FISH

(Fiji)

SERVES 4:

This is a touch taught by the French.

4 fillets of a white fish such as sole, haddock, flounder (each large enough for 1 serving)
1 medium-sized onion, minced

½ cup of grated Cheddar cheese
1 teaspoon of salt
¼ teaspoon of pepper
1 cup of tomato puree

Butter a baking dish and arrange the fillets in one layer. In a bowl, blend the onion, cheese, salt, pepper and tomato puree and pour over the fish. Bake, uncovered, in a preheated 350-degree oven for 40 minutes, or until the fish flakes easily when tested with a fork.

BAKED FISH

(Hong Kong)

SERVES 4 TO 6:

2 pounds of fillets of halibut, cod or haddock cut into 8 uniform pieces
1 teaspoon of salt
½ teaspoon of pepper
1½ teaspoons of minced fresh ginger root
1½ teaspoons of sugar
½ cup of chicken broth

8 large fresh mushrooms, cut into strips
4 slices of mildly smoked bacon, cut into strips the same size as the mushroom strips
4 scallions, cut on the diagonal in 2-inch pieces
2 tablespoons of butter

Sprinkle the fish pieces with salt, pepper, ginger and sugar. Place the broth in a large baking dish and arrange the fish, in one layer, in the dish. Cover each piece of fish with equal portions of the mushrooms and bacon strips and the scallions. Dot with butter and bake, uncovered, in a preheated 400-degree oven for 8 minutes. Baste the fish and cook for another 8 minutes. Fish is ready when it flakes easily when tested with a fork. Serve from the baking dish.

TAHITIAN BAKED FISH

SERVES 6:

6 tablespoons of butter, melted
2 teaspoons of soy sauce
Juice of 1 lemon
6 (½-pound) whole fish of your choice (trout are excellent)

1½ teaspoons of ground ginger
6 sheets of aluminum foil large enough to completely encase each fish
1 pound of fresh spinach leaves

In a small bowl, blend the butter, soy sauce and lemon juice and liberally brush each fish, inside and out, with the mixture. Sprinkle the inside of the fish with ginger and lightly sprinkle the top. On each sheet of foil (the islanders use broad tropical leaves, but foil does an even better job) arrange a base of spinach leaves with the fish on top, then more spinach over the fish. Wrap snugly in the foil, turning the ends in and folding it securely. Place in a shallow baking dish in one layer, and cook, uncovered, in a preheated 350-degree oven for 40 minutes. Serve in the foil for each guest to unwrap at the table.

BAKED CHICKEN HALIBUT

(Alaska)

SERVES 6:

These small, firm white-fleshed fish are the pride of Alaskans, many preferring them to their famous salmon. The fish does grow to an enormous size, but the small ones are a delicacy.

1 (5-pound) chicken halibut, cleaned and left whole	1 large sheet of aluminum foil, large enough to lay the whole fish on
1 teaspoon of salt	1 tablespoon of olive oil
½ teaspoon of pepper	¼ cup of whole fresh tarragon leaves
½ teaspoon of Hungarian paprika	

½ cup of melted butter
½ cup of dry white wine } blended

Sprinkle the fish, inside and out, with the salt, pepper and paprika. Rub the sheet of foil with the oil and place it in a shallow baking dish. Place the halibut on top, sprinkle evenly with the tarragon, and, basting every 5 minutes with the melted butter and wine, bake, uncovered, in a preheated 350-degree oven for 40 minutes, or until the fish flakes easily when tested with a fork.

FISH IN LIME JUICE

(*Tahiti*)

SERVES 8:

3 pounds of 1½-inch-thick halibut steaks, cut into ¼-inch-thick slices, then each slice cut in pieces 1½-inch square

1½ cups of fresh lime juice, strained

1 cup of chopped white onion

2½ teaspoons of salt

4 large, ripe tomatoes, peeled and chopped

1 cup of chopped scallions, including the green tops

3 hard-cooked eggs, coarsely chopped

In a bowl, blend well the fish pieces, lime juice, onion and salt. Cover and marinate in the refrigerator for 5 hours, while the fish "cooks" in the lime juice. Drain the fish well, place in a serving bowl and gently toss with the tomatoes, scallions and eggs.

OYSTERS AND BUTTERED EGGS

(*Australia and New Zealand*)

SERVES 4:

6 eggs
Pinch of cayenne
3 tablespoons of heavy
cream
12 fresh oysters, each cut
into 3 pieces

2 tablespoons of butter
1 teaspoon of salt
½ teaspoon of pepper

In a bowl, beat the eggs, cayenne and heavy cream.
Blend in the oysters. In a saucepan or frypan, melt the
butter, pour in the egg-oyster mixture and cook over
medium heat, stirring, for about 8 minutes, or until the
eggs are still soft and creamy, seasoning to taste with
the salt and pepper. Serve over hot buttered toast.

KADAVU FISH

(*Fiji and Tahiti*)

SERVES 4:

*Variations on this theme are served throughout the
South Sea Islands.*

6 tablespoons of butter
2 cups of cooked rice
2 tablespoons of flour
10 tablespoons of coconut
milk (see Baked Pa-
paya Tahiti)
4 cups of cooked, flaked
fish

2 small eggs, beaten
1½ teaspoons of salt
½ teaspoon of pepper
2 medium-sized onions,
minced

Butter a mold with 2 tablespoons of the butter and
line it with a thin layer of the rice, saving enough rice
to cover the top of the dish. In a saucepan, melt the

remaining 4 tablespoons of butter and blend with the flour into a smooth paste, gradually stirring in the coconut milk. Stir in the fish, eggs, salt, pepper and onion. Blend well and simmer for 5 minutes. Spoon the fish mixture into the rice-lined mold and cover with the remaining rice. Place in a shallow pan with 1 inch of hot water and cook, uncovered, in a pre-heated 350-degree oven for 30 minutes.

BLACK BEAN SAUCE WITH SHRIMP
(*Hong Kong*)

SERVES 6:

This is a famous Hong Kong specialty, the sauce with such a persuasive personality that it is always listed first and is used with shrimp, crab, lobster, fish and clams.

3 tablespoons of black beans, well rinsed (these salted fermented beans are available in specialty shops)

2 cloves of garlic, minced
2 tablespoons of peanut oil

1 tablespoon of soy sauce ⎫
1 tablespoon of dry sherry ⎬ blended
1 teaspoon of sugar ⎭

1 cup of chicken broth

1 teaspoon of minced fresh ginger root

3 tablespoons of water ⎫
1 tablespoon of corn- ⎬ blended
starch ⎭

1½ pounds of fresh shrimp, shelled and cleaned

With a mortar (or bowl) and pestle, make a smooth paste of the black beans and garlic. In a wok or saucepan, heat 1 tablespoon of the peanut oil and stir-fry the beans for 40 seconds. Stir in the blend of soy sauce, sherry and sugar and stir-fry for 40 seconds. Stir in the chicken broth and ginger. Bring to a boil, stir in the blend of cornstarch and water, and cook, stirring, until thickened. Pour over cooked shrimp.

TO COOK SHRIMP

In a wok or saucepan, heat the remaining 1 tablespoon peanut oil, add the shrimp, and over high heat stir-fry for 2 minutes. They should be firm but tender (shrimp can be cooked much more quickly than is commonly realized).

JAPANESE POTTED OYSTERS

SERVES 4:

1 cup of brown bean paste (available in specialty shops)	1 cup of bean curd, cut in small chunks
3 tablespoons of soy sauce	6 small scallions, cut into 2-inch lengths
2 tablespoons of grated fresh ginger root	½ pound of fine buckwheat noodles
6 cabbage leaves, coarsely chopped	½ cup of *fou* (croutons)
	24 oysters, out of their shells

In a pot, over medium heat, combine bean paste, soy sauce and ginger, stirring to break it up as it gets hot. Add the cabbage, bean curd, scallions, noodles and *fou*, and cook, stirring, for 5 minutes. Stir in the oysters, cooking just until their edges curl. Bring to a boil, remove from heat immediately and serve.

FIJI BAKED SHRIMP

SERVES 6:

3 cups of cleaned, shelled
raw shrimp
2 cups of Fiji Cream
Sauce (see Baked Pa-
paya Tahiti for coconut
milk recipe, then pro-
ceed as below)

2 cups of bread crumbs

Arrange the shrimp in one layer in a shallow baking dish and evenly spoon the cream sauce over the
shrimp. Sprinkle with the bread crumbs and bake, uncovered, in a preheated 350-degree oven for 40 minutes, or until bubbling and browned.

FIJI CREAM SAUCE

2 tablespoons of butter
3 tablespoons of minced
scallion
4 tablespoons of minced
red pepper

2 cups of coconut milk
(see Baked Papaya Ta-
hiti for recipe)
½ teaspoon of salt
2 tablespoons of corn-
starch

In a saucepan, melt the butter and sauté the scallion
and pepper until soft. Pour in 1½ cups of the coconut
milk and bring to a boil. Reduce sauce to a simmer. In
a bowl, mix the remaining ½ cup of coconut milk with
the salt and cornstarch and stir into the simmering
sauce. Cook, stirring, for 5 minutes.

FIJI CURRIED PRAWNS

SERVES 6:

2 tablespoons of butter
1 medium-sized white
  onion, chopped
2 tablespoons of curry
  powder
1 ounce preserved ginger,
  sliced, or ½ teaspoon of
  powdered
1 small chili pepper, sliced
1 teaspoon of salt
½ cup of beef broth

2 small cucumbers, peeled,
  cut lengthwise, seeds
  removed, then cut into
  ½-inch dice
2 tablespoons of lime juice
⅛ teaspoon of cayenne
1 cup of coconut milk (see
  Baked Papaya Tahiti)
4 cups of shelled, cooked
  shrimp

In a deep saucepan, melt the butter and sauté the onion until soft. Stir in the curry powder, ginger, chili pepper, salt and beef broth. Simmer for 3 minutes, stirring. Add the cucumbers, lime juice, cayenne and coconut milk, then simmer for 3 minutes longer. The cucumbers should be crisp, not soft. Stir in the shrimp, bring to a simmer, and serve immediately over boiled rice with a searing chutney.

PEPPERED SHRIMP

(Hong Kong)

SERVES 4:

1½ pounds of large shrimp,
  in shells
3 tablespoons of peanut
  oil
2 cloves of garlic, minced
3 chili peppers, minced

1-inch piece of fresh
  ginger root, shredded
2 scallions, minced
½ cup of the shrimp stock
2 tablespoons of Chinese
  chili sauce

Bring salted water to boil in a pot. Cook the shrimp 5 minutes. Drain, saving ½ cup of the water in which they cooked. When the shrimp are cool enough to handle, shell and clean them. In a wok or saucepan, heat the oil and fry the garlic, peppers, ginger and scallions for 4 minutes. Add the reserved shrimp stock, the shrimp and the chili sauce, blending well. Cook, stirring, for 5 minutes. No thickener is used, the sauce is supposed to be thin and peppery-hot.

SHRIMP WITH HEARTS OF PALM

(*Hawaii*)

SERVES 6:

3 tablespoons of peanut oil

1 medium-sized onion, minced

1 small green bell pepper, cored, seeded and minced

1 ripe tomato, peeled and chopped

1 teaspoon of salt

½ teaspoon of pepper

½ teaspoon of dry dillweed

2 large cans of hearts of palm, reserve liquid and cut the hearts of palm into 2-inch pieces

1½ pounds of raw shrimp, peeled and cleaned

In a large saucepan, heat the oil and sauté the onion and bell pepper until soft. Stir in the tomato, salt, pepper, dillweed and the liquid from the cans of hearts of palm. Blend well, cover and simmer for 10 minutes, then for 5 minutes, uncovered. Add the shrimp, cover and cook for 5 minutes, or until the shrimp are pink and firm but not hard. Stir in the cut-up hearts of palm and bring to a simmer to warm through. Taste for seasoning. Serve over rice.

TAHITI CURRIED SHELLFISH

SERVES 8:

This is finger food in the islands. The big freshwater prawns are cooked in their shells, the guests suck out the succulent flavor, break the shells and eat the tender white meat with their fingers.

1 cup of butter
4 medium-sized onions, minced
4 cloves of garlic, minced
½ teaspoon of salt
1 tablespoon of curry powder

32 large shrimp, in shells, rinsed and drained
1 cup of sweetish white wine

In a large saucepan, melt the butter, stir in the onion, garlic, salt and curry, sautéing until the onions are

soft. Add the shrimp and wine, blending well with the
curried onions and garlic. Cover the pan and simmer
for 15 minutes. Taste for seasoning. Serve over boiled
rice with the pan sauce.

HAWAIIAN FRIED SHRIMP

SERVES 6:

1½ pounds of shrimp, cleaned and deveined, but with tails intact	1½ cups of flour 3 small eggs, beaten 1½ cups of Chinese rice stick noodles, crumbled
1 teaspoon of salt ½ teaspoon of pepper	3 cups of cooking oil

Sprinkle the shrimp with salt and pepper. Dredge
them with flour (shaking off any excess), dip in the
beaten eggs, then roll in the crumbled rice noodles,
coating well. In a pot, wok or deep-fryer heat the oil
and fry the shrimp, 6 at a time, until crisp and lightly
browned. Drain on paper towels and serve warm.

SIMPLE JAPANESE SHRIMP TEMPURA

SERVES 6:

1½ cups of flour 1 teaspoon of salt 2 large eggs, beaten 1 cup of milk	2½ pounds of large raw shrimp, shelled and cleaned, but with tails intact; slit shrimp down the back but do not cut through 3 cups of cooking oil

In a bowl, blend well the flour, salt, eggs and milk,
making a thin batter. Press the shrimp flat into a
butterfly shape. Dip the shrimp into the batter and
fry in a pot, wok or deep-fryer in hot, but not smoking,
fat, a few at a time (do not crowd). Fry shrimp for

2½ to 3 minutes. Drain and serve with a sauce of your preference. Care should be taken to make the frying swift, the shrimp should be golden on the outside, moist and tender inside.

SALMON BAKED IN A BAG

(*Alaska*)

SERVES 6:

½ teaspoon of salt
½ teaspoon of pepper
½ cup of soft butter   } blended together into a
½ garlic clove, minced   paste
Juice of ½ a lemon
1 (6-pound) whole sal-
  mon, cleaned

Using all of the paste, slather the salmon inside and out. Place it in a heavy brown paper bag, fold it shut; lay the bag in the center of a shallow baking dish. Cook in a preheated 350-degree oven for 40 minutes,

or until the fish flakes easily with a fork. This is a
favorite Alaskan method of cooking salmon fresh from
the water. The wonderful fish steamed in a vapor of
its own juices emerges from the bag tender, moist and
pink. This dish is usually served with Matanuska Valley oversized fresh green peas and new potatoes in
butter.

SALMON CASSEROLE

(New Zealand)

SERVES 4:

1 cup of elbow macaroni
1 tablespoon plus 1 tea-
   spoon of salt
6 tablespoons of butter
1 pound of salmon,
   either canned or
   cooked fresh, bones
   removed, flaked
2 small onions, chopped

2 tablespoons of chopped
   pimiento
3 tablespoons of flour
2 cups of milk
½ teaspoon of pepper
1 teaspoon of Worces-
   tershire sauce
1½ cups of a grated pasta
   cheese to your liking

Cook the macaroni in plenty of boiling water with
1 tablespoon of salt, until almost tender, still a little
chewy. Drain well. Using 2 tablespoons of the butter,
grease a 2-quart casserole and spoon the macaroni
evenly into it. Add the salmon, gently mixing it into
the pasta. In a saucepan, over medium heat, melt the
remaining 4 tablespoons butter and cook the onion
until soft. Add the pimiento and cook 1 minute. Stir
in the flour, then, gradually, a small amount at a time,
stir in the milk, cooking and stirring until you have a
smooth, thick sauce. Blend in the 1 teaspoon salt, pepper, Worcestershire sauce and cheese; stirring well,
bring to a simmer. Taste for seasoning. Pour over the
macaroni and salmon in the casserole. Bake, uncovered, in a preheated 350-degree oven for 20 minutes, or until bubbling and browned.

SALMON STEAKS WITH
ALASKA KALE

(Alaska)

SERVES 6:

1 cup of water
2 teaspoons of salt
1 large bunch of fresh
   kale, discard stems, wash
   and drain
8 tablespoons of butter
1 teaspoon of pepper
6 salmon steaks, ¾ inch
   thick, each weighing
   about 8 ounces

½ cup of flour
1 tablespoon of olive oil
2 tablespoons of fresh
   lemon juice
1 tablespoon of fresh
   chopped tarragon

In a large pot, bring the water to a boil. Add 1 teaspoon of the salt and the kale, cover and cook 20 minutes, or until the kale is tender. Drain well, chop and mix with 3 tablespoons of the butter and ½ teaspoon of the pepper. Keep warm. Season the salmon with the remaining 1 teaspoon of salt and ½ teaspoon of pepper and lightly dredge with flour. In a saucepan, heat the remaining 5 tablespoons of butter and the oil and evenly brown the salmon on both sides. Cook 6 minutes on each side, or until the fish flakes easily with a fork. Evenly cover the bottom of a hot serving dish with the kale. Arrange the steaks on the bed of kale. Sprinkle them with lemon juice and tarragon.

NORTHWEST SALMON STEAK

(*Alaska*)

SERVES 4:

2 (1-pound) salmon steaks
½ teaspoon of salt
2 tablespoons of butter
4 slices of lean bacon
1 clove of garlic, minced
1 large onion, chopped

2 medium-sized ripe to-
matoes, peeled and
coarsely chopped
1 tablespoon of olive oil
½ teaspoon of dry oregano
Dash of Tabasco sauce

Sprinkle the salmon lightly with salt and place in a baking dish that has been greased with the 2 tablespoons of butter. Space the slices of bacon evenly across the fish. In a bowl, combine and blend well the garlic, onion, tomatoes, olive oil, oregano and Tabasco. Spoon this mixture over the fish, not too thickly; the remainder spoon around the sides of the salmon. Cook, uncovered, in a preheated 375-degree oven for 25 minutes, or until the fish flakes easily when tested with a fork.

FIJI FRIED FISH

SERVES 4:

2 pounds of fillets of sole,
cut into pieces 1½ inches
square
⅓ cup of soy sauce
⅔ cup of milk
⅓ cup of flour
1 egg, beaten
2 teaspoons of baking
powder
⅓ cup plus 1 tablespoon of
cornstarch

1 teaspoon of salt
½ teaspoon of pepper
Cooking oil for deep-
frying
1 (1-pound) can of pine-
apple chunks, with syrup
¼ cup of sugar
¼ cup of water

In a bowl, marinate the fish in the soy sauce for 1

hour, turning the pieces several times. In another bowl, blend the milk, flour, egg, baking powder, the ⅓ cup of cornstarch, salt and pepper, stirring and blending to the consistency of heavy cream. Pour the cooking oil in a pot, wok or deep-fryer to the depth of 2 inches and heat. Drain the fish pieces, dip quickly into the batter and cook, a few pieces at a time, for 2 minutes, or until the fish is crisp and golden. Drain on paper towels and keep warm. In a saucepan, pour in the pineapple with its syrup, add the sugar and bring to a gentle simmer. Blend the 1 tablespoon of cornstarch and water and gradually stir into the simmering pineapple until thickened. Place the pineapple in its sauce on a deep hot serving dish, arrange the fish on top of it and serve immediately.

SWEET AND SOUR FRIED FISH

(Hong Kong)

SERVES 6:

4 egg yolks
5 tablespoons of corn-
starch
2 tablespoons of dry sherry

1 teaspoon of salt
6 fillets of sole
1 cup of bread crumbs
3 cups of peanut oil

In a bowl, blend well the egg yolks, cornstarch, sherry and salt, mixing into a batter. Dip the fillets into this, then dredge with the bread crumbs. In a wok, pot or deep-fryer, heat the oil until very hot but not smoking. Fry the fish for 8 minutes, or until crisp and golden. Drain, keep warm and prepare the sweet and sour sauce.

SWEET AND SOUR SAUCE

5 tablespoons of butter
⅔ cup of chicken broth
7 tablespoons of cider
vinegar

5 tablespoons of sugar
2 tablespoons of ketchup
2 tablespoons of fresh
minced ginger root

2 tablespoons of corn-
starch
⅓ cup of water

} blended

In a saucepan, melt the butter and stir in the broth, vinegar, sugar, catsup and ginger. Bring to a simmer, stir well, then stir in the blended cornstarch and water, simmering and stirring until thickened. Pour the sweet-sour sauce over the fish, serving both sauce and fish very hot.

FILLETS OF SOLE IN COCONUT MILK

(Australia)

SERVES 4:

4 fillets of sole	2 cups of milk
1 teaspoon of salt	2 large onions, thinly
½ teaspoon of pepper	sliced
1 tablespoon of butter	3 large tomatoes, thinly
1 cup of grated coconut	sliced

Sprinkle both sides of the fillets with salt and pepper. Using the 1 tablespoon of butter, grease a baking dish and arrange the fish in one layer. Rinse the coconut under cold running water, then place it in a saucepan with the milk. Bring to a rolling boil; remove from the heat and let stand for 30 minutes. Place the coconut milk in an electric blender and blend on high for 30 seconds. Strain, pushing contents against the side of the strainer. Cover the fillets with the onions, then the tomatoes. Pour the coconut milk over the fish and vegetables, and bake, uncovered, in a preheated 375-degree oven for 40 minutes, or until the fish flakes easily when tested with a fork.

AUSTRALIAN GOLD COAST WHITING

SERVES 6:

2½ tablespoons of butter
4 large fresh mushrooms, sliced
6 large fillets of whiting
1 teaspoon of salt

½ teaspoon of pepper
½ cup of dry white vermouth
1 cup of bread crumbs

In a large, broiler-proof saucepan, melt 1 tablespoon of butter, add the mushrooms and sauté 3 minutes. Season the fillets with salt and pepper on both sides and arrange on top of the mushrooms in one layer. Pour in the vermouth; bring to a boil, cover, then lower the heat and simmer for 10 minutes, or until the fish flakes easily when tested with a fork. In another saucepan, melt the remaining 1½ tablespoons of butter and toss the bread crumbs in it. Sprinkle the buttered crumbs atop the fillets and place under the broiler until crisp and golden brown.

4
Poultry

"Poultry," wrote a famous epicure, "is for a cook what canvas is for a painter."

That was the remark of a Frenchman, but it could sum up the creative feeling of the people of the Pacific for poultry. In Hong Kong they cook chicken with "golden needles," tiger lily buds; in Hawaii they coat chicken with honey; in Tahiti they poach poultry in coconut cream; in Alaska they pair partridge with sauerkraut and in Australia they run a rabbit through a sweet and sour sauce.

It all adds up to an exciting adventure in cooking—and dining. Or should we be more specific and say, "Thanks, Pacific!"

HONOLULU STUFFED BREAST
OF CHICKEN

SERVES 6:

10 tablespoons of butter
6 tablespoons of minced onion
6 tablespoons of minced celery
6 tablespoons of cooked, mashed taro (or potato)

2 egg yolks, beaten
Salt
½ teaspoon of pepper
2 teaspoons Bell's Poultry Seasoning
3 whole chicken breasts, skinned, boned and separated in 6 portions

2 tablespoons of light brown sugar
6 tablespoons of whole cranberry sauce

} mixed together

In a saucepan, melt 6 tablespoons of the butter and sauté the onion and celery for 8 minutes, or until soft. Remove from heat and blend in well the mashed taro, egg yolks, 1 teaspoon of salt, pepper and poultry seasoning. Place the chicken breasts under wax paper and, using a wooden mallet, carefully flatten them to half again their size, without breaking or tearing the flesh. Place equal portions of the taro blend on each breast and evenly spread it. Spread the cranberry mixture atop the taro stuffing. Carefully roll up the breasts, jelly roll fashion, and tie into compact rolls. Refrigerate for 2 hours. This will give the rolled chicken form and substance. In a baking dish, melt the remaining 4 tablespoons of butter, arrange the chicken breasts in it, moving them around in the butter, then turning them over so they are buttered on all sides. Lightly sprinkle with salt and bake in a preheated 325-degree oven for 40 minutes, or until the breasts are golden brown and fork tender.

HAI YOOK PAR GAI

(*Hong Kong Chicken with Crab*)

SERVES 4 TO 6:

1 tablespoon of Chinese Five Spices Powder	2 (2½-pound) chickens, cut up
1½ teaspoons of salt	3 cups of peanut oil
6 tablespoons of cold water	
8 tablespoons of corn-starch	} blended in a bowl

Blend Five Spices with the salt and rub the mixture well into the chicken pieces. Let the chicken set at room temperature for 1 hour. In a wok, pot or deep-fryer, heat the oil until very hot, but not smoking. Dip the chicken pieces into the cornstarch batter and fry, a few pieces at a time, until golden brown. Drain on paper towels (but keep warm) while the crab sauce is being prepared.

CRAB SAUCE

3 tablespoons of peanut oil	8 ounces of crabmeat, flaked
1 teaspoon of grated fresh ginger root	Salt and pepper to taste
8 scallions, finely sliced	2 egg whites, slightly beaten
1 cup of chicken broth	
1 tablespoon of cornstarch	} blended
1 tablespoon of water	

In a saucepan, heat the oil and sauté the ginger and scallions for 1 minute. Stir in the chicken broth and crabmeat, season with salt and pepper, bring to a boil, and gradually stir in the egg whites. As it sets in floating shreds, stir in the mixture of cornstarch and water. Cook, stirring, until thick. Pour the sauce over the chicken and serve immediately.

HONG KONG GOLDEN NEEDLE CHICKEN

SERVES 4 TO 6:

6 large dried black
Oriental mushrooms
(available in specialty
shops)

1½ dozen dried golden
needles (dried Tiger
Lily buds, available in
specialty shops)

4 tablespoons of peanut
oil

2 (2½-pound) broiler
chickens, cut up

1½ teaspoons of salt

4 tablespoons of dry
sherry

2 tablespoons of soy
sauce

2 teaspoons of grated
fresh ginger root

6 canned water chest-
nuts, minced

2 cups of chicken broth

4 scallions, with tops,
thinly sliced on the
diagonal

In separate bowls, cover the mushrooms and golden
needles with water and soak for 2 hours. Drain, rinse
with cold water and squeeze dry. Slice the mushrooms
thinly; cut the needles into 1-inch lengths. In a large

saucepan, heat the oil. Season the chicken with salt and brown it evenly in the oil, a few pieces at a time, adding more oil, if necessary. Return all of the browned chicken to the saucepan, adding the sherry, soy sauce, ginger, water chestnuts, mushrooms, golden needles and the chicken broth. Cover and simmer for 12 minutes, or until the chicken is fork tender. Taste for seasoning. Stir in the scallions and cook for 3 minutes. Serve the chicken in its sauce.

SMALL CHICKEN LUAU

(Hawaii)

SERVES 4:

1 (3-pound) chicken, cut up
2 teaspoons of salt
¼ cup of flour
4 tablespoons of butter
¾ cup of water
¼ cup of shredded coconut

1 cup of hot milk
1½ pounds of fresh spinach, washed and shredded into ½-inch pieces
1 small onion, minced

Sprinkle the chicken with 1 teaspoon of the salt and lightly dredge with flour. In a saucepan, melt the butter and brown the chicken evenly. Add ½ cup of the water, cover the pan and simmer for 25 minutes, or until chicken is fork tender. In a small pot, combine the coconut and the hot milk, let it marinate for 20 minutes, then bring it to a simmer and cook for 10 minutes. Drain, discarding the milk, saving the coconut. In a pot, bring the remaining ¼ cup of water to a boil. Add the spinach, onion and remaining 1 teaspoon salt. Cook for 5 minutes, drain. Stir the cooked coconut and the spinach with onion into the saucepan with the chicken. Bring to a simmer, cover and cook for 5 minutes. Taste for seasoning.

JAPANESE CHICKEN LOAF

SERVES 8:

This is a simple, tasty Oriental version of a meat loaf. The Japanese serve this hot in their homes and cold on picnics.

8 dried mushrooms, soaked in water 20 minutes, drained and minced
6 ounces of bamboo shoots, minced
5 scallions, minced
½ cup of bread crumbs
2 tablespoons of sake or dry sherry
2 teaspoons of sugar
1 teaspoon of salt
4 tablespoons of soy sauce
2 eggs, beaten
2 pounds of boned chicken, dark and light meat, minced
1 tablespoon of sesame seeds

In a bowl, blend well all ingredients except the sesame seeds. Place in a buttered loaf pan, sprinkle with the sesame seeds and cook, uncovered, in a preheated 350-degree oven for 50 minutes, or until the thin blade of a knife can be inserted in the center of the loaf and withdrawn clean.

TAHITIAN CHICKEN REA

SERVES 6 TO 8:

3 (2- to 2½-pound) broiler chickens, cut up
2 teaspoons of salt
1 teaspoon of pepper
5 tablespoons of butter
2 tablespoons of cooking oil

3 medium-sized onions, thinly sliced
3 cloves of garlic, minced
3 cups of Thick Fiji Coconut Cream (see Fiji Fish Appetizer)
1 teaspoon of turmeric

Season the chicken pieces well with salt and pepper. In a large saucepan, heat the butter and oil and brown the chicken evenly. Transfer the chicken to a casserole. Add the onion and garlic to the pot the chicken was browned in and sauté until soft. Cover the chicken with the onion and garlic, cover the casserole tightly and cook for 1 hour in a preheated 325-degree oven, or until the chicken is tender. Mix the coconut cream with the turmeric, stir it into the chicken pot and bring to a simmer on top of the stove. Stir and serve immediately.

TAHITI TAMARIND CHICKEN

SERVES 8:

2 teaspoons of salt
3 cloves of garlic
} mashed into paste

1 teaspoon of ground coriander
1 teaspoon of ground ginger
2 teaspoons of sugar
½ teaspoon of pepper

1 cup of tamarind water (see Pacific Potatoes with Tamarind Sauce)
3 (2-pound) chickens, cut up
3 cups of cooking oil

In a large bowl, blend the garlic-salt paste, coriander, ginger, sugar, pepper and tamarind water.

Add the chicken and toss it until well coated. Marinate for 4 hours in the refrigerator, occasionally turning the pieces of chicken. Drain and dry the chicken. In a pot, wok or deep-fryer, heat the oil and deep-fry the chicken for about 10 minutes, a few pieces at a time, until they are crisp and evenly browned. Drain on paper towel.

SPICY ROAST CHICKEN THIGHS

(Hong Kong)

SERVES 6:

⅓ cup of peanut oil
3 tablespoons of dry sherry
½ cup of soy sauce
3 cloves of garlic
1½ teaspoons of salt

1 tablespoon of Chinese Five Spices Powder
1 teaspoon of minced fresh ginger root
12 medium-sized chicken thighs

In a large bowl, blend the oil, sherry and soy sauce. Mash the garlic with the salt. Add it, the Five Spices and the ginger to the bowl. Blend well. Add the chicken to the mixture, turning to evenly coat it, and marinate for 4 hours, turning several times during this time. In a roasting pan, arrange the chicken thighs, skin side up. Spoon 3 tablespoons of the marinade over them, and basting every 15 minutes with the marinade, roast, uncovered, in a preheated 350-degree oven for 1 hour, or until the thighs are crisply brown on the outside and tender inside.

DICED CHICKEN WITH WALNUTS
(Hong Kong)

SERVES 4:

4 tablespoons of peanut oil	2 egg whites, slightly beaten
½ pound of walnut meats	1 teaspoon of sugar
½ teaspoon of salt	1 (3-pound) chicken, skinned, meat removed from bones, cut into bite-sized pieces
1 tablespoon of cornstarch	
1 tablespoon of soy sauce	
2 tablespoons of sherry	

In a saucepan or wok, heat the oil and stir-fry the walnut meats until just lightly browned. Be careful, they burn quickly. Remove walnuts. In a bowl, blend well the salt, cornstarch, soy sauce, sherry, egg whites and sugar. Dip the chopped chicken into the sauce and evenly brown in the oil in the saucepan or wok in which the walnuts were cooked. This should take about 4 minutes. Do not overcook the chicken. The morsels should be tender and moist inside, golden brown outside. Stir the cooked walnuts into the chicken in the saucepan or wok and serve very hot.

AUSTRALIAN SWEET AND SOUR RABBIT (or Chicken)

SERVES 4:

Although chicken can be used for this dish, rabbit is classic.

1 teaspoon of salt
½ teaspoon of pepper
1 (3½-pound) rabbit (or chicken), cut up
1 tablespoon of butter
¼ cup of hot water
¼ cup of brown sugar
2 tablespoons of cornstarch
¼ cup of cider vinegar
1 cup of pineapple juice (juice drained from canned pineapple can be used)

½ tablespoon of soy sauce
1 small green pepper, seeded, cored and sliced
1 stalk of celery, scraped and chopped
4 scallions, chopped
1 (20-ounce) can of pineapple pieces, drained

Salt and pepper the rabbit pieces. In a pot, melt the butter and over medium heat, evenly brown the rabbit. Pour in the hot water, cover the pot and simmer, stirring occasionally, for 25 minutes, or until the rabbit is tender (add more water, if necessary). In a saucepan, blend the brown sugar, cornstarch, vinegar, pineapple juice and soy sauce, and simmer, stirring until slightly thickened. Pour this mixture over the rabbit, and simmer, uncovered for 5 minutes. Add the green pepper, celery and scallions, cover and simmer for 5 minutes. Stir in the pineapple pieces, simmering until they are hot. Taste for seasoning. Serve with rice. The vegetables should be crisp.

CHICKEN LIVERS WITH COCONUT CREAM SAUCE

(Fiji)

SERVES 6:

3 tablespoons of cooking oil

1½ pounds of chicken livers

1 teaspoon of salt

2 small tomatoes, peeled and diced

1½ cups of Fiji Cream Sauce (see Fiji Baked Shrimp)

In a saucepan, heat the oil, add the livers, sprinkle them with salt and sauté for 5 minutes, or until they are firm (but not hard, do not overcook) and lightly browned. Stir in the tomatoes and the cream sauce; bring to a boil, then a simmer. Stir well and serve.

GINGER DUCK

(Hong Kong)

SERVES 6:

4 cups of minced raw duck meat, preferably from the breast

8 scallions, with tops, coarsely chopped

3 tablespoons of sake or dry sherry

2 teaspoons of minced fresh ginger root

1½ tablespoons of corn-starch

1 teaspoon of salt

3 tablespoons of peanut oil

In a large bowl, blend all of the ingredients except the oil. Let stand at room temperature for 45 minutes. In a wok or large saucepan, over high heat, heat the oil. Stir in the duck mixture and stir-fry for 3½ minutes, or until duck bits are firm. Taste for seasoning.

HONOLULU HONEY DUCK

SERVES 4:

This uncomplicated, never-fail method always rates raves.

4 tablespoons of honey
2 tablespoons of soy sauce
1 tablespoon of sugar
2 tablespoons of sake or
   dry sherry

2 tablespoons of Hoisin
   Sauce (available in
   specialty shops)
1 (5-pound) duck
1 teaspoon of salt

In a large bowl, blend all the ingredients except the duck and salt. Place the duck in a deep dish and coat it well with the honey sauce. Cover the dish and let the duck marinate 8 hours. Turn it occasionally and spoon the sauce over it. Season the inside of the duck with salt and set it on a rack in a roasting pan. Roast, uncovered, in a preheated 325-degree oven for 35 minutes. Cover with foil and roast for 45 minutes. Raise the oven heat to 425 degrees, remove the foil and roast for 15 minutes longer or until tender.

ALASKAN BROILED WILD DUCK

SERVES 4:

In their classically simple style, Alaskans present a duck tasty as any labored over by a three-star French chef.

2 wild ducks, split into halves	1 teaspoon of salt ½ teaspoon of pepper
3 tablespoons of soft butter 1 tablespoon of lemon juice	} blended (to rub ducks with)
12 thin strips of salt pork, ⅛ inch wide	
1 cup of melted butter Juice of 2 lemons	} blended (to baste ducks with)

Season the ducks with salt and pepper and rub well with the mixture of butter and lemon juice. Drape each half duck with 3 strips of salt pork. Place on a broiler pan, and basting every 3 minutes with the melted butter and lemon juice mixture, broil 25 minutes or until tender. These ducks will be slightly pink when the tender stage is reached.

It is important that wild ducks "season" for 4 days in the refrigerator before they are cooked.

PTARMIGAN (or Cornish Game Hen) AND SAUERKRAUT

(Alaska)

SERVES 6:

Here is an outstanding blending of the bounty of the northern state, with a coupling of wild white partridge and onions and cabbages, which are kings of the cold country.

3 tablespoons of butter
1 tablespoon of olive oil
2 (2½-pound) ptarmigan
  (if you use Cornish
  game hens, use 1 for
  each person), cleaned
  and trussed
Salt and pepper

2 medium-sized onions,
  chopped
1 clove of garlic, minced
1 quart of fresh sauerkraut,
  well drained
1 teaspoon of caraway
  seeds
1 teaspoon of pepper
1 pint of dry white wine

In a deep pot large enough to hold birds and sauerkraut, heat the butter and oil, and over medium heat, evenly brown the birds, seasoning them with salt and pepper. Remove them from the pot and stir in the onion and garlic and sauté until soft, stirring up the brown particles on the bottom of the pot. Add the sauerkraut, caraway seeds, pepper and wine, blending well with the onion and garlic. Cover the pot, bring to a boil, then to a simmer, and cook on top of the stove for 20 minutes. Add the ptarmigan (or game hens), pushing them well into the sauerkraut, cover and bake in a preheated 325-degree oven for 1 hour, or until the birds are fork tender.

5
Meat

Meat. The heart of any cookbook. The main offering around which everything else is built. Despite such variety as Polynesian Pork with Pineapple, Marinated Moose Steaks, New Zealand Curry of Lamb, Japanese Beef Steak Teriyaki and Hong Kong Roast Suckling Pig, there is a single word to sum up this chapter: Spectacular! Here are offerings to spark the most jaded of appetites.

AOTEAROA STEAK
(*New Zealand*)

SERVES 6:

3 pounds of blade steak (beef), cut into 2-inch cubes

2 tablespoons of brown sugar

1 cup of dry red wine
½ cup of tomato juice
⅔ cup of cider vinegar
Juice of 1 lemon
} stirred together in a measuring cup

2 tablespoons of grated lemon rind

2 tablespoons of chopped bacon

2 tablespoons of flour

1½ teaspoons of curry powder

½ teaspoon of ground ginger

2 tablespoons of grated Cheddar cheese

In a large casserole, place the beef and sprinkle in the sugar, flour, curry powder and ginger. Pour the wine-tomato juice-vinegar-lemon juice mixture around the sides of the pot. Sprinkle the lemon rind, bacon and cheese. Cover and cook in a preheated 325-degree oven for 2 hours, or until the beef is tender.

AUSTRALIAN CARPETBAG STEAK

SERVES 4:

1 (2-pound) piece of sirloin strip steak

1½ teaspoons of salt

½ teaspoon of pepper

8 large, plump oysters

3 tablespoons of melted butter

1 teaspoon of lemon juice

1 teaspoon of sherry

Make a slit down the center of the steak, halfway through the meat. Season with salt and pepper. Insert

the oysters in the pocket in the steak. Brush the surface of the steak and oysters with the melted butter and broil to taste, rare, medium or well-done. When broiled to your taste, remove the steak from broiling pan and stir the remaining melted butter, lemon juice and sherry into the steak juices in the pan. Place under the broiler until simmering and spoon over the steak with its stuffing of oysters.

FIJI COCONUT BEEF CAKES

Serves 8:

2 pounds of ground beef
⅛ teaspoon of ground
cumin
2 cloves of garlic, minced
2½ teaspoons of ground
coriander

2 teaspoons of salt
1 teaspoon of pepper
2 small eggs, beaten
5 cups of finely grated
coconut
2 cups of cooking oil

In a large bowl, place all ingredients except the cooking oil. Blend thoroughly, then stir vigorously with a spoon into a fluffy consistency. Form into oblong patties, ½-inch thick and about 2 inches in diameter. Heat the cooking oil in a deep saucepan until very hot, but not smoking (oil should be 1 inch deep). Cook about 6 cakes at a time for 4 minutes on each side, or until brown and crisp. Drain on paper towels and serve with an interesting rice dish.

BEEF ROLLS

(*Hawaii*)

Serves 4:

2 tablespoons of butter
1 pound of ground beef
½ cup of shredded pine-
apple
1 tablespoon of minced
onion
1 tablespoon of tomato
sauce
2 teaspoons of salt
½ teaspoon of pepper

1 pound of potatoes,
peeled, boiled, well
drained and mashed
½ cup of self-rising flour
1 egg, beaten
1 tablespoon of minced
parsley
1 egg, beaten (to brush
tops of rolls before bak-
ing)

In a large saucepan melt 1 tablespoon of the butter. Add the beef, pineapple, onion, tomato sauce, 1 teaspoon of the salt and the pepper. Cook over low heat, stirring, for 10 minutes, or until the beef has lost its pink color. In a bowl, blend well the potatoes, the remaining 1 tablespoon butter, flour, the remaining 1 teaspoon salt, 1 beaten egg and the parsley. Place on a floured pastry board and work into a soft dough, then roll out into a sheet ¼-inch thick, and cut the sheet into 3-inch squares. Place a spoonful of the meat mixture on the squares just off center, moisten the edges with water and carefully fold, pressing the edges with a fork, sealing the meat in. Place on a greased baking sheet. Brush the tops with beaten egg and bake in a preheated 400-degree oven for 15 minutes, or until golden brown.

DAU TSAI NGAU

(Hong Kong Beef with String Beans)

SERVES 4 TO 6:

- ¾ cup of chicken broth
- 1½ teaspoons of sugar
- 1½ tablespoons of cornstarch
- 3 tablespoons of soy sauce
- ⅓ cup of peanut oil
- 2 slices of fresh ginger root, shredded
- 2 cloves of garlic, minced
- ½ teaspoon of salt
- 1½ pounds of boneless sirloin, cut into ⅛-inch-thick slices, ½ inch wide, 1 inch long
- 6 scallions, with tops, cut into 1-inch pieces
- 1½ cups of bamboo shoots, shredded
- 8 dried Oriental mushrooms, soaked in water 1 hour, drained and shredded
- 1 pound of fresh, tender, slender string beans
- 3 tablespoons of dry sherry

In a bowl, blend well the chicken broth, sugar, cornstarch and soy sauce, set aside. In a wok or pot, heat half of the oil, add the ginger, garlic and salt and, over medium heat, cook until lightly browned. Add the beef, increase the heat to high, stir-fry the beef until it is lightly browned. Transfer the beef to a hot bowl. Add the remaining oil to the wok, and stir-fry the scallions, bamboo shoots, mushrooms and string beans for 2 minutes. Pour in the sherry, cover and cook 1 minute. Return the beef to the wok, stir in the chicken broth-soy sauce mixture and cook over high heat, stirring, until sauce has thickened.

STIR-FRIED BEEF WITH SNOW PEAS
(Hong Kong)

SERVES 6:

1½ pounds of rump steak, partially frozen, so it can be cut paper-thin, then shredded

1 teaspoon of salt

3 tablespoons of soy sauce

4 tablespoons of peanut oil

6 Oriental dried mushrooms, soaked in water for 1 hour, drained and shredded

8 scallions, cut into 1-inch pieces

¾ cup of beef broth

2 tablespoons of dry sherry

1 teaspoon of sugar

1½ tablespoons of corn-starch

1 tablespoon of water

} blended

12 ounces of snow peas, stringed, blanched for 1 minute in salted, boiling water, then drained

In a bowl, toss together the shredded beef, salt and soy sauce, mixing well. Marinate for 1 hour. In a wok or pot, heat 2 tablespoons of the oil and stir-fry the beef for 1½ minutes. Transfer the beef to a hot bowl. Add the remaining 2 tablespoons oil to the wok and

heat. Add the mushrooms and scallions, cook 1½ minutes. Stir in the beef broth, sherry and sugar, bring to a boil, blend in the cornstarch-water mixture, cooking until the sauce begins to thicken. Stir in the beef and snow peas; cook 30 seconds, or until heated through.

SUKIYAKI

(Japan)

SERVES 6:

The world's finest beef, called shimofuri (fallen frost) is, almost without argument, from Japan. Fed beer, massaged with gin, fattened on rice, rice bran and beans, the three-year-old steers end up on tables as "Kobe" beef. This is Japan's most famous dish. In Tokyo, the Japanese also use pieces of chicken breast as a change from beef. There are as many different recipes for sukiyaki in Japan as there are for beef stew in the U. S. This one is typical.

About 4 ounces of beef suet

2 pounds of filet, sliced wafer-thin, then cut into bite-sized pieces

1 tablespoon of sugar

6 tablespoons of light soy sauce

½ cup of sake (dry sherry can be used, but try to get the rice wine, available in most liquor stores)

½ pound of chrysanthemum leaves (or spinach) in bite-sized pieces

6 bamboo shoots, sliced lengthwise ⅛-inch thick

½ pound of small fresh mushrooms, sliced lengthwise ⅛-inch thick

2 small white onions, thinly sliced

12 ounces of *shiraraki* (fine noodles), cooked and drained

1 (¾-pound) block of *tofu* (bean cake) cut into bite-sized cubes

12 whole, medium-sized scallions, cut diagonally into 2-inch lengths

6 eggs, each beaten in a dipping bowl

You will be cooking in stages, so everything remains hot, with guests coming back for more. Therefore, cook about one-third of the meat, vegetables, etc. at a time.

At the table, in a special sukiyaki pan, or a heavy frypan, on a portable table grill (Ronson makes a good one), melt one-third of the suet. When it sizzles, add the beef slices, turning and cooking until they are lightly browned. Sprinkle lightly with sugar, soy sauce and sake, then add the chrysanthemum leaves (or spinach), bamboo shoots, mushrooms, onion and noodles. Place the vegetables each in its own corner in the pan, turning them and the beef to warm. Sprinkle the vegetables and noodles very lightly with sugar, soy sauce and sake. This cooking should take no more than 5 minutes, the beef should be pink. Now add the bean cake and scallions, and cook another 5 minutes, spooning the liquid in the pan over everything as the food cooks. This is a continual cooking, with guests helping themselves, even cooking the sukiyaki. Plain boiled rice is served, and each guest gets a bowl of the beaten egg to dip his beef and vegetables in. It is important that all food is bite-sized, and chopsticks are also a must.

The light soy sauce, noodles and bean cake are available in Oriental specialty shops.

STUFFED LAMB CHOPS
(New Zealand)

SERVES 6:

6 (2-inch-thick) loin lamb chops with sides slit deeply to make pocket for stuffing

1 teaspoon of salt
½ teaspoon of pepper } blended
¼ teaspoon of rosemary

2 tablespoons of butter
½ pound of *kumaras* or sweet potatoes, cut into small dice
2 small white onions, chopped
6 slices of bread, trimmed of crusts, dried 20 minutes in a low oven, then diced

2 small eggs, beaten
⅛ cup of milk
1 tablespoon of chopped parsley
½ teaspoon of salt
¼ teaspoon of pepper

Sprinkle the chops with the blended salt, pepper and rosemary. Melt the butter in a saucepan and cook the potatoes and onion until soft. Off heat stir in the bread, eggs, milk and parsley, salt and pepper, mixing well. Spoon the stuffing into the pocket in the chops and close with toothpicks or skewers. Place in a baking dish and cook, uncovered, in a preheated 350-degree oven for 40 minutes, or until tender.

BEEF TERIYAKI

(Japan)

SERVES 6:

A Kobe sirloin steak is as tender as an American beef fillet. The Japanese often just broil steaks on their compact charcoal grills, the hibachi, but most of them prefer it with a sauce, teriyaki.

8 tablespoons of soy sauce	2 teaspoons of grated fresh ginger root
5 tablespoons of sugar	
8 tablespoons of sake or dry sherry	2 pounds of shell steak, cut into ¼-inch-thick strips
2 cloves of garlic, minced	
½ lemon, thinly sliced	

In a bowl, blend the soy sauce, sugar, sake (or sherry), garlic, lemon and ginger. Marinate the steak strips in this sauce for 2 hours. Drain, and cook quickly over charcoal, or in a small amount of cooking oil in a frypan. Quickly is the key word; the steak slices should be pink inside, and are much better underdone than overdone.

NEW ZEALAND GRILL

SERVES 4:

8 (1-inch-thick) loin
  lamb chops
1½ teaspoons of salt
½ teaspoon of pepper
8 thick slices of bacon
2 medium-sized potatoes,
  cut into ¼-inch-thick
  slices

½ cup of cooking oil
3 tomatoes, cut into thick
  slices
½ cup of seasoned bread
  crumbs

Season the chops with salt and pepper and wrap well in the bacon slices. Place on a large broiler rack. Dip the potato slices in oil, sprinkle with salt and pepper and arrange on the broiler rack. Broil 6 minutes; turn the chops and potatoes. Dip the tomato slices in oil, dredge with bread crumbs. Place on the rack beside the chops and broil 6 minutes, or until the chops are cooked to your taste.

TOKOMARU BAY LAMB CHOPS
(New Zealand)

SERVES 4:

8 (1-inch-thick) rib lamb
  chops
1 teaspoon of salt
½ teaspoon of pepper
2 tablespoons of butter
1 tablespoon of olive oil
2 small onions, chopped

2 small cloves of garlic,
  minced
1 small bay leaf, crushed
2 teaspoons of fresh lemon
  juice
½ cup of dry white wine

Season the chops with salt and pepper. In a casserole, heat the butter and oil and brown the chops on both sides. Add the onion and garlic and cook until soft. Add the bay leaf, lemon juice and wine and stir. Cover the pot and cook in a preheated 350-degree oven for 15 minutes, or until the chops are cooked to your taste.

CURRY OF LAMB
(Australia and New Zealand)

SERVES 8:

4 pounds of lean lamb from leg, cut into 1½-inch cubes

1 cup of flour
1½ teaspoons of salt } blended
½ teaspoon of pepper

4 tablespoons of butter
1 tablespoon of oil
3 medium-sized onions, chopped
2 tablespoons of curry powder
¼ teaspoon of ground ginger

4 medium-sized apples, peeled, cored and diced
2 cups of beef broth
1 tablespoon of tomato paste
2 tablespoons of heavy cream

Dredge the lamb cubes with the seasoned flour. In a heavy pot, heat the butter and oil and brown the lamb evenly. Add the onion and cook for 5 minutes. Stir in the curry powder and ginger. Cook 3 minutes. Add the diced apples, broth and tomato paste and stir. Cover the pot and cook in a preheated 325-degree oven for 1 hour, or until the lamb is tender. Stir in the cream. Taste for seasoning.

WELLINGTON LAMB STEW
(*New Zealand*)

SERVES 6:

2 tablespoons of butter
1 tablespoon of cooking oil
1 (5-pound) shoulder of lamb, trimmed of fat and cut into 2-inch cubes
1½ teaspoons of salt
½ teaspoon of pepper
3 medium-sized onions, thinly sliced

3 large carrots, scraped and sliced
2 cups of beef broth
1 cup of dry red wine
½ cup of rice
1 (10-ounce) package of frozen peas, defrosted
¼ pound of fresh, small mushrooms, quartered

In a large, heavy pot, heat the butter and oil and brown the lamb evenly, seasoning with salt and pepper. Pour off fat; cook the onion 5 minutes, then stir in the carrots, beef broth and wine. Simmer, covered, for 1 hour, or until lamb is almost tender. Stir in the rice and cook, uncovered, for 10 minutes. Add the peas and mushrooms and cook 5 minutes. Taste for seasoning.

NEW ZEALAND GOOSE

SERVES 6:

Never let it be said that the settlers of New Zealand didn't have a sense of humor. They called this dish "stuffed goose" or "colonial goose."

2 cups of bread crumbs
1 small egg, beaten
2 teaspoons of salt
1 teaspoon of pepper
½ teaspoon of dry sage
½ teaspoon of dry thyme

1 tablespoon of chopped parsley
4 tablespoons of butter
2 medium-sized onions, chopped
1 (5-pound) leg of lamb, bone removed

In a bowl, blend bread crumbs, egg, 1 teaspoon of
salt, ½ teaspoon of pepper, sage, thyme and parsley.
In a saucepan, melt 2 tablespoons of the butter and
sauté the onion until soft. Add the onions and their
butter to the bowl with the bread crumbs and herbs.
Mix well with a fork. Fill the cavity in the lamb leg,
rub outside of leg with remaining 2 tablespoons butter and season with remaining 1 teaspoon of salt and
½ teaspoon pepper. Place the leg on a rack in a roasting pan. Cook, uncovered, in a preheated 350-degree
oven for 2 hours, or until the lamb is tender and
cooked to your taste, basting at intervals.

LAMBS' LIVER IN WHITE WINE AND SOUR CREAM

(*New Zealand*)

SERVES 4:

2 lambs' livers, cut into
½-inch-thick slices

1 cup of flour
1½ teaspoons of salt   } blended
½ teaspoon of pepper

2 tablespoons of cooking   1 cup of dry white wine
  oil   1½ cups of sour cream
1 tablespoon of butter   Juice of 1 lemon
2 medium-sized onions,
  sliced

Dredge the liver slices with the seasoned flour. In
a frypan, heat the oil and brown the liver evenly.
Remove and keep warm. Pour off the oil from the
frypan, melt butter and sauté the onion until soft.
Pour in the wine, stir, raise the heat and cook 5 minutes, or until the wine is reduced by half. Stir in the
sour cream, lower heat and bring to a simmer (do
not boil or the sour cream will curdle). Stir in the
lemon juice and pour the sauce over the liver.

MARINATED MOOSE STEAKS
(or Beef Strip Sirloin)
(Alaska)

SERVES 4:

4 (1-inch-thick) moose
sirloin steaks (or beef
strip sirloin), each
weighing about ½ pound

3 cups of dry red wine
3 cloves of garlic, halved } mixed into a marinade
½ cup of soy sauce

5 tablespoons of butter   Salt and pepper to taste
1 tablespoon of olive oil   2 tablespoons of brandy

In a deep dish, marinate the steaks in the wine-garlic-soy sauce mixture for 5 hours, occasionally turning them. Drain and dry the steaks well. In a large frypan heat one-half of the butter and the oil. When sizzling, add the steaks, season with salt and pepper and brown on one side, turn, season and cook over medium heat for 5 minutes. Turn again and cook for 2 minutes. Test for doneness by cutting into a steak with a sharp knife. They should be moist and pink inside. Transfer the steaks to a hot serving platter and keep warm. Pour off the grease from the frypan, but retain the brown specks left in the bottom of the pan. On high heat, melt the remaining butter in the frypan, stir in the brandy, scraping the bottom of the pan to release the brown specks and simmer for 30 seconds. Spoon the brandy pan-sauce over the steaks and serve.

POLYNESIAN PORK AND PINEAPPLE
(*Tahiti*)

SERVES 8:

3 pounds of fresh lean
pork shoulder, cut into
2-inch pieces

2 cloves of garlic, minced

1½ teaspoons of salt

1 teaspoon of pepper

½ teaspoon of ground
ginger

8 sheets of aluminum
foil, 12 inches long

1 16 oz. can of pine-
apple chunks, drained

2 large green peppers,
seeded, cored and each
cut into 8 pieces

8 small potatoes, peeled

In a bowl, blend well the pork, garlic, salt, pepper
and ginger. On each sheet of foil arrange the pork,
pineapple, peppers and potatoes in equal amounts.
Bring the corners of the foil together and twist to form
8 well-sealed packages. Place on a baking sheet and
cook in a preheated 350-degree oven for 2 hours.

BROCCOLI AND PORK IN
OYSTER SAUCE
(*Hong Kong*)

SERVES 6 TO 8:

2 teaspoons of sugar

2 tablespoons of corn-
starch

⅔ cup of chicken broth

⅓ cup of oyster sauce

⅓ cup of peanut oil

4 slices of fresh ginger
root, shredded

2 cloves of garlic, minced

½ teaspoon of salt

2 pounds of lean pork, cut
into ⅛-inch-thick slices,
½ inch wide, 1 inch long

2 bunches (about 3
pounds) of broccoli,
leaves discarded, stems
peeled, flowerets split in
half

½ cup of water

In a bowl, blend well the sugar, cornstarch, chicken

broth and oyster sauce, then set aside. In a wok or pot, heat the oil, add the ginger, garlic and salt and cook until lightly browned. Increase heat, add the pork and stir-fry until the pork is lightly browned. Stir in the broccoli and stir-fry for 3 minutes. Add the water, cover and cook for 3 minutes. Pour in the chicken broth-oyster sauce mixture, stir and cook on the high heat until the mixture thickens. Reduce the heat, cover and cook for 2 minutes.

LUAU OR KALUA PORK
(*Hawaii*)

SERVES 10:

This substitute is not as impressive as the whole steamed suckling pig brought out of the luau pit, but no one but a luau master and a pit perfectionist will complain. This recipe has a touch of our Deep South.

1 (8-pound) fresh ham
  (carefully remove and
  save the rind)

3 tablespoons of coarse
  salt   ⎫
1 tablespoon of bourbon
  whiskey   ⎬ blended
1 tablespoon of minced
  fresh ginger root
2 tablespoons of soy sauce ⎭

Enough cornhusks to   Aluminum foil
cover the pork in a
thick layer (in Hawaii ti
and banana leaves are
used)

Score the ham and rub in the salt-bourbon-ginger-soy sauce mixture. Wrap the ham completely in the cornhusks, tying them tightly on so the ham is well

sealed. Wrap snugly in the foil, place on a rack in a
roasting pan and cook in a preheated 500-degree oven
for 30 minutes. Lower the heat to 400 degrees and
cook the ham for 4 hours. During the last 30 minutes
of cooking time add the pork rind to the rack in the
roasting pan. It should emerge crisply browned when
the ham is finished. If it is not brown enough, return
the rind to the oven, raise the heat to 500 degrees
and cook until it is crisply brown, but watch carefully.
Serve pieces of the crisp rind with the pork, which is
usually cut into bite-sized pieces and served in com-
munal bowls so it can be eaten by hand.

PORK FRIED RICE
(Hong Kong)

SERVES 6:

You can use this as a tasty accompaniment to an-
other dish and cook it without meat, or you can cook
it with meat as they do in Hong Kong and still con-
sider it an accompaniment dish. The Chinese vary the
meat, using everything from bacon bits to chicken,
but with pork the favorite.

2 tablespoons of peanut oil	2 cloves of garlic, minced
	5 whole scallions
1½ cups of lean cooked pork, cut into ½-inch dice	3½ cups of cooked rice

2 eggs
4 tablespoons of soy
sauce   } beaten together
¼ teaspoon of ground
ginger

In a wok or saucepan, heat the oil and brown the
pork evenly. Stir in the garlic and stir-fry until soft.
Slice thinly, on a slant, the white part of the scallions,

then the green tops, keeping them separate. Add the white part to the pork and garlic and stir-fry for 3 minutes; then add the green parts and cook 2 minutes. Both should be crisp. Stir in the cooked rice. When hot and well blended with the pork, add the beaten egg mixture. Stir-fry until the eggs are set.

HONG KONG ROAST SUCKLING PIG

SERVES 6:

1 (10-pound) suckling pig, well washed and dried
3 teaspoons of salt
½ teaspoon of pepper
½ cup of flour

2 tablespoons of peanut oil
2 tablespoons of sugar
½ cup of honey
¼ cup of soy sauce
½ cup of chicken broth

Season the pig inside and out with the 1 teaspoon of the salt, the pepper, and evenly dust the outside

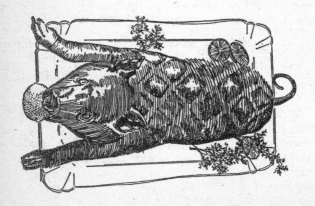

with the flour. In a saucepan, blend the oil, sugar, the remaining 2 teaspoons of salt, honey, soy sauce and chicken broth, and, stirring, bring to a simmer. Brush the pig liberally with this mixture and place on a rack in a large roasting pan. Skewer the forelegs forward, the hind legs back. Roast, uncovered, in a preheated 450-degree oven for 20 minutes. Reduce the heat to 350 degrees and roast 25 minutes to the pound, basting with the honey mixture every 10 minutes. If the ears brown too quickly, cover with well-buttered brown paper or aluminum foil. Traditionally, the pig is served on a large platter, facing the guest of honor. Its crisp skin has been cut in a crisscross pattern, in 2-inch long strips. These are pulled off and eaten first, then the pig is carved and apportioned.

POLYNESIAN PORK CHOPS

(New Zealand)

SERVES 6:

2 tablespoons of butter	¼ cup of dark brown
1 (10-ounce) can of	sugar
crushed pineapple	6 (1-inch-thick) loin
4 medium-sized *kumaras*	pork chops
or sweet potatoes,	1½ teaspoons of salt
sliced	½ teaspoon of pepper

Butter a large casserole and layer the pineapple on the bottom. Arrange the potatoes in a layer on the pineapple, then sprinkle with brown sugar. Arrange the pork chops on top of the sugar, seasoning with salt and pepper. Cover the casserole and cook in a preheated 350-degree oven for 1½ hours, or until potatoes and chops are almost tender. Uncover the casserole and cook for 10 minutes or until the chops are brown and tender.

ISLAND SPARERIBS

(Hawaii)

SERVES 6:

½ cup of sake or dry sherry
1 tablespoon of grated
   fresh ginger root
½ cup of soy sauce
½ cup of tomato ketchup
½ cup of dark brown sugar

2 teaspoons of salt
3 cloves of garlic, minced
½ teaspoon of Chinese Five
   Spices Powder
3 pounds of small lean
   spareribs

In a deep saucepan, blend well all the ingredients except the spareribs. Bring to a boil, stirring well. Place the spareribs in a large, flat dish, pour the blended sauce over them and let the ribs marinate at room temperature for 4 hours, turning occasionally to keep them evenly coated. Arrange the ribs on a large baking pan, and bake, uncovered, in a preheated 350-degree oven for 50 minutes, or until tender and crisply brown. Baste the ribs well with the marinade every 10 minutes. Serve with "hot" mustard (dry Coleman mustard mixed with a small amount of cold water into a semithick sauce).

FIJI SWEET POTATO PUDDING

SERVES 6:

6 large sweet potatoes,
   peeled and grated
Meat from 2 medium-
   sized coconuts, grated

1 cup of Thick Fiji Coco-
   nut Cream (see Fiji Fish
   Appetizer)
1 teaspoon of salt
1 tablespoon of butter

In a bowl, blend potatoes, coconut meat, coconut cream and salt. Butter a baking dish with the 1 tablespoon of butter and spoon the potato mixture into it. Cook, uncovered, in a preheated 400-degree oven for 40 minutes. This is a good accompaniment for pork dishes.

VENISON (or Beef) SIRLOIN
WITH CIDER

(Alaska)

SERVES 6:

4 tablespoons of butter
2 tablespoons of flour
2 cups of beef broth
2 tablespoons of tomato
puree
2 tablespoons of wine
vinegar
1 teaspoon of molasses
⅛ teaspoon of ground ginger
Salt and pepper to taste

2 tablespoons of cooking
oil
1 (3-pound) piece of top
sirloin of venison (or
beef)
4 medium-sized onions,
thinly sliced
2 cloves of garlic, minced
1 to 2 cups of sweet cider
1 bay leaf
⅛ teaspoon of thyme

In a saucepan, melt 2 tablespoons of the butter, stir
in the flour and cook, stirring constantly, until smooth
and slightly golden. Add the broth, a small amount at
a time, stirring until the sauce is smooth. Stir in the
tomato puree, vinegar, molasses and ginger. Season
with salt and pepper. Set aside. Heat the oil and
remaining 2 tablespoons butter in a casserole and
brown the venison on both sides. Pour off all but 2
tablespoons of fat, add the onion and garlic and cook
until the onion is soft. Stir in the prepared sauce, plus
1 cup of cider, the bay leaf and thyme. Blend. Cover
and bring to a boil on top of the stove, then place in a
preheated 350-degree oven for 1½ hours, or until meat
is tender, adding more cider if liquid cooks off.

6
Vegetables

What can you expect from people who can grow 70-pound cabbages, four-foot-tall rhubarb, beans a yard long, give turnips and pumpkins glamour, sauerkraut personality, create fritters from coconuts, dumplings from bananas and call carrots "sunshine food?"

You'd expect an exceptional offering of vegetable recipes. And you'd be right.

BANANA DUMPLINGS
(*Fiji*)

SERVES 4:

4 large green bananas,
peeled and grated

1½ teaspoons of salt
3 cups of milk

In a bowl, blend the bananas and salt, then form into small balls or dumplings. In a pot, bring the milk to a boil, then reduce to a simmer. Lower the dumplings on a tablespoon into the milk and cook for 25 minutes. These are good with roast meats.

PACIFIC YARD-LONG BEANS
(Fiji and Tahiti)

SERVES 6:

Asiatic beans can grow four feet long, yet the beans, only ¼-inch wide, have a unique flavor, which accounts for their other name "asparagus beans."

4 tablespoons of peanut oil	6 cups of yard-long beans, cut into 2-inch pieces
4 tablespoons of shrimp paste or anchovy paste	½ teaspoon of molasses
1½ cups of coconut milk (see Baked Papaya Tahiti)	1 tablespoon of soy sauce

In a saucepan, heat the oil over medium heat. Blend in the shrimp (or anchovy) paste and coconut milk. Keeping at a simmer, stir in the beans, molasses and soy sauce. Bring to a boil, stir well, lower heat, cover and cook for 7 minutes, or until the beans are just tender, but still firm. Taste for seasoning. Do not overcook; beans should be a bit crunchy.

CHICKEN AND BEAN SPROUTS
(Hong Kong)

SERVES 6:

2 tablespoons of peanut oil	1 whole cooked chicken breast (preferably poached in chicken broth), cut into slivers
5 cups of fresh mung-bean sprouts	4 tablespoons of soy sauce
	1 teaspoon of sugar

In a saucepan or wok, heat the oil over high heat. Stir in the bean sprouts and chicken slivers. Cook, stirring, for 1 minute. Stir in the soy sauce and sugar and cook, stirring, for 1 minute longer. Sprouts should be very crisp (overcooking makes them limp and spoils the flavor). Taste for seasoning.

TAHITIAN BAKED BREADFRUIT

SERVES 6 TO 8:

Captain Bligh (yes, the same Mutiny on the Bounty Bligh) was so impressed with this dish and the round-ish, prickly yellowish-green fruit that can weigh as much as 10 pounds, that in 1792 he brought it to Jamaica from Tahiti.

1 tablespoon of cooking oil	1 teaspoon of pepper
1 ripe breadfruit	1 cup of melted butter
2 tablespoons of salt (dependent on size of breadfruit)	6 to 8 wedges of fresh lime

If you can, charcoal-bake this over gray coals for 1½ hours. If not, grease a baking pan with the cooking oil and cook the breadfruit, whole, in a preheated 350-degree oven for 1 hour or more. It is cooked when a knife blade inserted into its center emerges clean. Cut into quarters, remove the seeds, then cut the quarters into serving portions. Sprinkle with salt and pepper and pass on a serving plate with a bowl of melted butter and lime wedges.

CHINESE BROCCOLI
(*Hong Kong*)

SERVES 6:

4 tablespoons of peanut oil

1 (2-pound) bunch of fresh broccoli, peel large stalks and slice, break flowerets in half, peel small stems, cut into ½-inch pieces

6 large Oriental dried mushrooms, soaked 30 minutes in warm water, drained and sliced

4 bamboo shoots, cut into matchstick-sized slices

4 tablespoons of chicken broth

1 teaspoon of sugar

½ cup of cooked ham, sliced same size as the bamboo shoots

In a wok or pot, heat the oil and over high heat stir-fry the broccoli for 2 minutes. Add the mushrooms and bamboo shoots and stir-fry for 1 minute. Stir in the chicken broth and sugar, cover the pot and cook for 2 minutes. Before serving, stir in the ham and stir-fry for 30 seconds, or until hot.

BRUSSELS SPROUTS IN GAME STOCK
(*Alaska*)

SERVES 4 TO 6:

Alaska, a country that still is rich in game and fish of all kinds, may be the only state in the U. S. that officially closes schools during part of the hunting season so the children can help their parents replenish their meat larder. Thus, game is used in many ways with the other foods of the region, especially with the vegetables which grow so large that they are the envy of California gardeners.

4 cups of brussels sprouts	½ cup of grated Cheddar cheese
2 cups of rich game stock, caribou, moose or venison (or beef)	Salt and pepper to taste

Place the brussels sprouts in a baking dish, cover with the stock, cover the dish and bake in a preheated 375-degree oven for 15 minutes, or until the sprouts are cooked but still crunchy. Overcooking destroys their flavor. Sprinkle with the cheese and put under the broiler for 5 minutes, or until the cheese starts to brown. Taste for seasoning, but the stock and the cheese should provide enough for most tastes.

SUNSHINE CARROTS
(*Australia*)

SERVES 4:

6 medium-sized carrots, scraped and sliced crosswise 1-inch thick	¼ teaspoon of salt
	¼ teaspoon of ground ginger
1 tablespoon of sugar	¾ cup of fresh orange juice
1 teaspoon of cornstarch	2 tablespoons of butter

Cook the carrots in boiling salted water for 10 minutes. Reduce to a simmer and cook 10 minutes more, or until tender. Drain. In a saucepan, blend the sugar, cornstarch, salt, ginger and orange juice, and simmer, stirring, until mixture thickens. Stir in the butter and cook 1 minute. Pour the sauce over the carrots and gently toss.

CHINESE CELERY
(Hong Kong)

SERVES 4 TO 6:

¼ cup of peanut oil
6 large stalks of celery, scraped and sliced diagonally
4 small bell peppers, cored, seeded and cut into ¼-inch strips, then each strip cut in half

1 teaspoon of salt
1 tablespoon of soy sauce
⅓ cup of slivered almonds, toasted

In a saucepan, heat the oil. Stir in the celery and peppers. Cover the pan and cook over low heat for 6 minutes, or until the vegetables are cooked but still very crunchy. Blend in the salt, soy sauce and almonds. Taste for seasoning.

COCONUT FRITTERS
(Fiji)

SERVES 4:

1 cup of flour
½ teaspoon of salt
1½ teaspoons of baking powder
2 teaspoons of sugar
1 cup of grated coconut

2 tablespoons of butter
2 egg yolks, beaten
2 tablespoons of coconut milk (see Baked Papaya Tahiti)
2 cups of cooking oil

In a bowl, sift together the flour, salt and baking powder and blend in the sugar and coconut. Cut in the butter with a fork or pastry cutter; mix thoroughly. Blend in the egg yolks and coconut milk. Place on a floured pastry board and work until the dough is smooth. Roll out into a flat piece ½ inch thick, cut into 2 x 1-inch strips and fry in deep fat until crisp and golden.

BAKED LETTUCE
(New Zealand)

SERVES 8:

4 medium-sized, solid heads of Boston lettuce	4 tablespoons of flour
3 cups of boiling water	2 cups of medium cream
1 cup of boiling chicken broth	1 teaspoon of salt
	½ teaspoon of pepper
	Dash of Tabasco sauce
6 tablespoons of butter	¾ cup of bread crumbs

In a pot that the lettuce will fit snugly into, place the lettuce, pour the boiling water over it, let stand 5 minutes, then drain thoroughly, pressing each with a dry towel. Cut the heads into halves. In the same pot (without the water), arrange the lettuce, pour the chicken broth over it and cook, covered, over medium heat for 5 minutes, or until the lettuce is tender. Place in a colander and drain very well. In a saucepan, melt 4 tablespoons of the butter, add the flour and blend into a smooth golden paste. Over low heat, gradually stir in the cream, stirring until the sauce is smooth and has thickened. Stir in the salt, pepper and Tabasco and simmer 3 minutes. Butter a casserole, arrange the lettuce in it, cover with the cream sauce, sprinkle with the bread crumbs and dot with the remaining 2 table-spoons butter. Bake, uncovered, in a preheated 400-degree oven for 10 minutes, or until the sauce bubbles and the top is golden.

PACIFIC POTATOES WITH
TAMARIND SAUCE

(*Tahiti*)

SERVES 6:

⅓ cup of cooking oil

3 small sweet red peppers, cored, seeded and cut into strips ⅛ inch wide and 1 inch long

3 small onions, minced

2 cloves of garlic, minced

4 tablespoons of tamarind water

2 tablespoons of brown sugar

1½ teaspoons of minced fresh ginger root

1 teaspoon of salt
Cooking oil for deep-frying

5 medium-sized potatoes, peeled and cut into ⅛-inch-thick slices

In a saucepan, heat the oil and cook the peppers, onion and garlic for 5 minutes, or until soft. Stir in the tamarind water (made by soaking 3 ounces of tamarind pulp, available in stores that sell South Pacific items, in 1½ cups of boiling water for 1 hour, then rubbing it through a sieve to separate the seeds and fiber), brown sugar, ginger and salt. Cook, stirring, over high heat, until most of the liquid has evaporated and the mixture is thick. Keep warm. Pour 4 inches of oil into a pot, wok or deep-fryer and heat. Fry the potato slices by the handful, each frying for 7 minutes, or until the potatoes are crisp and evenly browned. Remove with a slotted spoon and drain on paper towels. When all the potatoes are cooked and drained, place them in a bowl with the red pepper and onion mixture, gently toss and serve.

DEEP-FRIED SWEET POTATOES
(*Fiji*)

SERVES 8:

2½ pounds of sweet
potatoes, peeled and
cut into wafer-thin
slices

3 cups of cooking oil
2 tablespoons of
confectioners' sugar

In a large bowl, place 1 cup of ice cubes and 2 cups of water. Add the potato slices and soak for 30 minutes. Drain and dry the potatoes thoroughly. Heat the oil in a pot, wok or deep-fryer and fry them in several batches, not crowding them in the fryer. Each frying should take about 4 minutes; the potato slices should be golden when properly fried. Drain the potatoes on paper towels, sprinkle with sugar and serve them while they are warm.

PUMPKIN PUDDING
(*Tahiti*)

SERVES 4:

1 medium-sized pumpkin, peeled and cut into chunks	1 cup of sugar
2 tablespoons of water	2 cups of Thick Fiji Coconut Cream (see Fiji Fish Appetizer)
1½ cups of flour	2 eggs, beaten
1 teaspoon of salt	1 tablespoon of butter

Over low heat, cook the pumpkin in the water until tender. Drain, place in a strainer or colander and drain overnight. Mash the pumpkin well, place it in a bowl and sift in and blend the flour, salt and sugar. Gradually stir in the coconut cream and the eggs. Butter a baking dish and evenly spoon in the pumpkin mixture. Cook, uncovered, in a preheated 400-degree oven for 40 minutes, or until set.

HAWAIIAN GLAZED PAPAYA

SERVES 6:

These unique slices of green papaya are used as an unusual accompaniment with pork dishes, giving even ordinary pork chops style.

5 small green papayas, peeled, halved lengthwise, seeded and cut into 1-inch-thick slices

½ cup of fresh lime juice ⎫
8 tablespoons of butter ⎬ warmed together and blended into a smooth mixture
1 cup of guava jelly ⎭

Place the papaya slices in a large baking dish in one layer, not overlapping. Bake in a preheated 350-

degree oven for 10 minutes, basting every 2 or 3 minutes with the lime juice mixture. Turn and basting, cook for another 10 minutes, or until the slices are tender and golden.

BRAISED SAUERKRAUT
(Alaska)

SERVES 8:

Alaska may no longer be the gold mining center of the world, but it could probably be called the cabbage capital. Few homes are without a cabbage patch; the vegetable seems to bloom in that climate, and the Alaskans cook it in numerous ways. Here's a favorite:

2½ pounds of fresh sauerkraut
½ pound of lean salt pork, cut into the thinnest possible slices to cover the bottom and sides of the cooking pot
3 cloves of garlic, minced
2 teaspoons of pepper
1 teaspoon of caraway seeds
3 cups of chicken broth
2 cups of dry white wine
4 medium-sized whole onions, peeled and nailed with 4 small whole cloves

Drain the sauerkraut, rinse well in cold water and squeeze out as much of the moisture as possible, without mashing the sauerkraut. With the salt pork slices, line the bottom and sides of a heavy pot. Fork half of the sauerkraut into the pot, seasoning with half of the garlic, half the pepper and half of the caraway seeds. Fork in the remaining sauerkraut, seasoning with remaining garlic, pepper and caraway. Pour in the chicken broth and wine. Push the onions with the cloves deeply into the sauerkraut. Cover the pot and cook in a preheated 325-degree oven for 2½ hours. Taste for seasoning. Alaskans use this as a vegetable, or combine it with cooked meats such as spareribs, pork sausages, sliced roast pork, pork hocks, or with pieces of wildfowl or game, and serve it as an impressive meal.

FIJI FRIED TAROS

SERVES 6:

8 medium-sized taros, peeled and cut into sticks 2 inches long and ¾-inch thick

4 cups of cooking oil
Salt

In a large bowl, half water, half ice cubes, soak the taro sticks for 20 minutes, or until very crisp. Drain and dry well. In a pot, wok or deep-fryer, heat the oil until very hot, but not smoking. Fry the taro sticks a few at a time until crisp and brown. Keep warm, sprinkle with salt and serve as quickly as possible. The Fijians like these with fried fish.

AUSTRALIAN TOMATO PIE

SERVES 4:

2 cups of bread crumbs
1 small onion, chopped
½ teaspoon of chopped fresh marjoram
1 teaspoon of chopped fresh thyme
1 tablespoon of chopped parsley
Juice of 1 lemon

1 teaspoon of salt
½ teaspoon of pepper
5 large, ripe tomatoes, peeled and cut into thick slices
1 tablespoon of butter

In a bowl, blend bread crumbs, onion, marjoram, thyme, parsley, lemon juice, salt and pepper. In a

large, deep pie plate, place a layer of tomato slices, cover with a layer of bread crumb mixture, another layer of tomatoes, finishing with a layer of bread crumbs. Dot with butter and bake, uncovered, in a preheated 325-degree oven for 40 minutes, or until tomatoes are cooked but not mushy.

BRAISED TURNIPS
(Alaska)

SERVES 6:

The Alaskans often cook their turnips as below, then surround roasting wildfowl, rabbit, ptarmigan, or horned game with the turnips just before the roasting is finished. The turnips, basted with the juices of the roasting meat are superb. I had an unforgettable serving of them braised with Dall sheep, perhaps the tastiest of all game. Ribs of beef, or pork, of course, can be substituted.

4 tablespoons of butter	½ teaspoon of pepper
2 cups of beef broth	2 pounds of small turnips,
½ teaspoon of salt	scraped and quartered

In a deep saucepan, melt the butter, then stir in the broth, salt and pepper. Bring to a boil, add the turnips, cover, reduce to a simmer and cook for 15 minutes, or until the turnips are tender but still firm. Do not overcook; mushy turnips are a disappointment. Taste for seasoning.

If you are going to finish braising the turnips with a roast, cook them on top of the stove for 8 minutes, then give them another 8 minutes in the roasting pan, basting them several times with the meat juices.

HAWAIIAN MIXED VEGETABLE FRY

SERVES 6 TO 8:

6 large dried Oriental mushrooms
¾ cup water
½ pound of green beans, French cut
4 small white onions, thinly sliced
4 small carrots, scraped and cut into 2-inch matchstick-thin strips
4 stalks of celery, scraped and sliced into ⅛-inch diagonal slices
3 tablespoons of peanut oil

¾ pound of snow peas, stems and string along sides removed
1 (4-ounce) can of bamboo shoots, drained and cut into matchstick-thin strips
½ pound of bean sprouts
2 tablespoons of chicken broth mixed with
2 tablespoons of soy sauce
1½ teaspoons of salt
½ teaspoon of pepper

Soak the mushrooms in the water for 30 minutes, drain, dry and thinly slice them. Place the green beans, onion, carrots and the celery in a colander and pour boiling water over them. Drain thoroughly. In a wok or saucepan over high heat, heat 1 tablespoon of oil; stir-fry the snow peas, bamboo shoots, mushrooms and bean sprouts for 1 minute. Remove and keep warm. Add the remaining 2 tablespoons oil to the wok and cook the green beans, onion, carrots and celery, stirring constantly, for 2 minutes. Return the snow peas, bamboo shoots, mushrooms and bean sprouts to the wok. Add the chicken broth and soy sauce mixture, salt and pepper. Cover the wok and cook on high heat for 1½ minutes. Stir and taste for seasoning and crunchiness. Vegetables should be crunchy-crisp. If more cooking is needed, make it brief.

7
Salads

Put *scallops* in a salad, make a salad dressing sauce from *peanuts*, roll bananas in *lime juice,* cook potatoes in *chicken broth?* That's the way they do it in the Pacific. It's not so crazy. Read on—

FIJI BANANA SALAD

SERVES 4:

4 ripe bananas, peeled
and sliced
3 carrots, scraped and
finely grated

⅔ cup of coarsely chopped
salted peanuts
4 tablespoons of
mayonnaise
Lettuce leaves

In a bowl, gently blend the bananas, carrots, peanuts and mayonnaise. Serve on crisp lettuce leaves.

TAHITIAN BANANAS

SERVES 4:

4 bananas, peeled, cut
into halves lengthwise,
then into thirds

3 tablespoons of fresh
lime juice
1 cup of minced peanuts
12 crisp lettuce leaves

Sprinkle the banana pieces with lime juice, roll in the minced peanuts and place in a salad bowl alternating with layers of the crisp lettuce.

MATANUSKA VALLEY BEET SALAD
(Alaska)

SERVES 6:

12 medium-sized beets

1 teaspoon of sugar
3 tablespoons of freshly
grated horseradish
¾ cup of sour cream
Salt and pepper to
taste
} blended into a salad
dressing

6 large crisp leaves of
lettuce

3 tablespoons of minced
parsley

Boil the beets in water until tender. Cool slightly, then rub off the skins. Slice into a salad bowl. Add the salad dressing and toss well. Serve on lettuce leaves, sprinkled with the parsley. This goes well with marinated moose steaks.

BEAN SPROUT AND CHICKEN SALAD
(Hong Kong)

SERVES 6 TO 8:

2½ pounds of fresh bean
sprouts

2 cups of shredded,
cooked chicken breasts

2 tablespoons of dry
mustard
1 teaspoon of salt
2 tablespoons of sesame
seed oil
4 tablespoons of wine
vinegar
4 tablespoons of soy
sauce

⎫ blended 4 hours before
serving ⎬

Fill a large pot two-thirds full of water and bring it
to a boil. Add the bean sprouts and cook for 2½ minutes. Drain the bean sprouts well and chill them.
Blend the chicken with the bean sprouts and 5 minutes before serving toss with the mustard sauce.

NAMASU SALAD
(Japan and Hawaii)

SERVES 6:

DRESSING

3 small egg yolks
1 teaspoon of *wasabi*
(Japanese horseradish)
½ cup of water

3 tablespoons of white
vinegar
1 tablespoon of sugar
1 tablespoon of cornstarch
½ teaspoon of salt

Place all ingredients in an electric blender for 30
seconds.

3 small carrots, scraped
and cut into thin strips
¼ of a medium-sized firm
head of white cabbage,
finely shredded

1 large *daikon* (a giant
Japanese white radish),
scraped and cut into
thin strips

In a large bowl, half filled with ice cubes and cold water, place the vegetables and chill for 40 minutes, or until very crisp. Drain and dry well and serve covered with the dressing.

SEA ISLANDS PEANUT SAUCE SALAD

(*Fiji, Tahiti*)

SERVES 6:

1 cup of shredded
cabbage
1 cup of thin, peeled
cucumber strips
1 large ripe tomato,
peeled and cut into
6 wedges
1 cup of cored, seeded
green pepper strips
1 cup of ½-inch papaya
chunks

1 cup of ½-inch pineapple
chunks
1 cup of avocado slices,
soaked in the juice of
½ a lemon
1 cup of ½-inch chunks of
peeled mango
Peanut Sauce (see
below)

PEANUT SAUCE

1 tablespoon of peanut oil
½ cup of freshly roasted,
finely ground peanuts
2 tablespoons of soy sauce
2 tablespoons of lime juice
1 tablespoon of molasses
Salt to taste

2 cloves of garlic, minced
½ cup of coconut milk or
water (see Baked
Papaya Tahiti)
⅛ teaspoon of dry red
pepper flakes

In a saucepan, heat the oil over medium heat, turn

heat low and add all of the remaining sauce ingredients, blending well, and simmer, uncovered, for 10 minutes. Cool, then blend with all of the above vegetables and fruits, tossing gently.

NEW POTATO SALAD
(*Alaska*)

SERVES 6:

Potatoes, like all of the rest of the vegetables from Alaska's Matanuska Valley are famous. Here's an Alaskan change-of-pace salad far from the sourdough's cabin kitchen.

18 small new potatoes with their skins
3½ cups of chicken broth
½ teaspoon of salt
2 large scallions, white part only, chopped
⅓ cup of chopped broad-leaf parsley

1 clove of garlic, minced
3 tablespoons of dry white wine
2 tablespoons of wine vinegar
½ cup of olive oil
Salt and pepper to taste

Simmer the potatoes in the chicken broth and salt, covered, until tender. Drain, cool slightly and peel the potatoes. Slice them into a bowl while they are still warm. Blend with all of the remaining ingredients. Taste for seasoning. It is important to do the blending while the potatoes are still warm so the seasonings permeate.

ONION CUCUMBER SALAD
(Japan)

SERVES 4:

5 small cucumbers (no longer than 2 inches), unpeeled and sliced wafer thin
6 scallions, chopped finely
3 tablespoons of soy sauce

2 tablespoons of sesame oil
4 tablespoons of white vinegar
1½ tablespoons of sugar
½ teaspoon of salt

Place all ingredients in a bowl, blend well and let marinate for 3 hours.

CHINESE PON PON SALAD
(Hong Kong)

SERVES 6:

6 large, crisp lettuce leaves
4 cups of shredded, cooked pork loin
4 scallions, with tops, chopped
2 cloves of garlic, minced
2 teaspoons of minced fresh ginger root

4 tablespoons of sesame paste
3 tablespoons of soy sauce
2 tablespoons of white vinegar
2 teaspoons of sugar
2 tablespoons of Chinese chili paste
2 tablespoons of sesame oil

On 6 salad plates, place a lettuce leaf. Arrange equal portions of the pork atop each. In a bowl, blend well the scallions, garlic, ginger, sesame paste, soy sauce, vinegar, sugar, chili paste and sesame oil. Spoon it over the pork on the lettuce leaves.

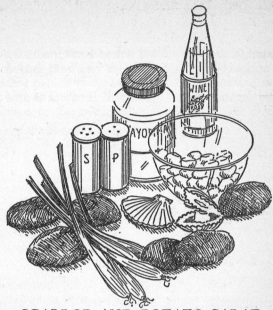

SCALLOP AND POTATO SALAD

(*Alaska*)

SERVES 6:

6 medium-sized potatoes
Salt and pepper
½ cup plus 2 tablespoons
  of dry white wine
½ cup of water

1½ pounds of scallops
  (if sea scallops cut in
  halves; if bay, leave
  whole)

1 cup of mayonnaise ⎫
6 scallions, with tops, ⎬ blended
  finely chopped ⎭

Boil the potatoes in their skins until they are tender,
but still firm. Cool slightly, peel and cut into ¼-inch-
thick slices. Place in a dish and lightly sprinkle with
salt and pepper and the 2 tablespoons of the wine. In
a saucepan, bring the ½ cup of wine and the water to

a boil. Reduce to a simmer, add the scallops and cook for 10 minutes, or until the scallops are firm but tender (do not overcook as they'll become tough). Drain and cool the scallops. Place potato slices and scallops in a salad bowl, blend by tossing gently with the mixture of mayonnaise and scallions. Taste for seasoning. Serve at room temperature; do not refrigerate.

SHRIMP AND GREEN BEAN SALAD
(Japan)

SERVES 4 TO 6:

12 large shrimp	5 tablespoons of white
1 pound of green beans,	vinegar
cut into 1-inch pieces	3 tablespoons of sugar
6 hard-cooked eggs	1 tablespoon of soy sauce
(remove and reserve	3 tablespoons of water
yolks)	2 tablespoons of
5 tablespoons of chicken	cornstarch
broth	
5 tablespoons of sake or	
dry white wine	

In a pot of boiling water, cook the shrimp in their shells for 5 minutes. Remove shrimp and reserve the water. When the shrimp are cool enough to handle, peel and cut them in half lengthwise. Cook the beans in the shrimp water for 6 minutes, then plunge them into ice-cold water. Drain. Slice the egg whites. In a salad bowl, combine the sliced egg whites, shrimp and beans. In a saucepan, blend well the chicken broth, sake (or wine), vinegar, sugar and soy sauce, and stirring, bring to a boil. Make a paste of the cornstarch and water and stir into the saucepan with the chicken broth mixture, simmering and stirring until the sauce is smooth and thick. Cool, pour over the shrimp, egg whites and beans and gently toss. Refrigerate for 2 hours. Serve the salad with crumbled egg yolks atop.

SOUTH PACIFIC SALAD
(*Australia*)

SERVES 6:

3 quarts of water

1 tablespoon plus 1 teaspoon of salt

6 (8-ounce) rock lobster tails

2 cups of shredded lettuce

½ teaspoon of pepper

1 (10-ounce) package of frozen peas and carrots, cooked according to the package directions and drained

4 tablespoons of mayonnaise

1 tablespoon of fresh lemon juice

2 pimientos, cut into strips

¼ cup of bottled capers, rinsed and drained

1 cucumber, peeled and sliced lengthwise

1 cup of black olives

3 medium tomatoes, quartered

1 avocado, peeled and sliced

In a pot, place the water and 1 tablespoon of the salt and bring to a boil. Add the lobster tails, cover and simmer for 10 minutes. Drain, cover with cold water and drain again. With kitchen shears, cut underside membrane from each tail, then extract the meat, saving the shells intact. Cut four slices from each tail, then chop the rest of the meat. Save the slices; toss the chopped lobster with shredded lettuce, 1 teaspoon salt, pepper, peas and carrots, 2 tablespoons of the mayonnaise and ½ tablespoon of lemon juice. Stuff the lobster shells with the mixture, decorate with the lobster slices and spread with the remaining mayonnaise. Refrigerate. To serve, arrange pimiento strips and capers atop each shell and garnish with cucumbers, olives, tomatoes and avocado, sprinkled with the remaining lemon juice.

8
Breads, Pastries, Desserts

From Sourdough Bread and Blueberry Flapjacks to Papaya Custard and Pineapple Snow, the
Pacific touch remains versatile and talented. Need
a new dessert? Try Grapefruit Alaska. Want an
after-dinner conversation maker? Offer New Zealand Pikelets and Lemon Honey. Interested in
raising a guest's eyebrow and tantalizing his taste
buds? Serve him Fiji Stuffed Bananas. And if you
want to create a new hero image for all of the
kids on your street, bake up a batch of Australian
Anzac cookies and let your generosity be your
guide.

ANZACS
(*Australia*)

MAKES ABOUT 3½ DOZEN COOKIES:

1 stick (¼ pound) of
butter
1 tablespoon of maple
syrup
1 cup of all-purpose flour
⅔ cup of sugar

½ teaspoon of baking
powder
1 cup of rolled oats
1 cup of dried coconut
½ teaspoon of vanilla

In a bowl, cream the butter with the maple syrup.
Blend in all of the remaining ingredients and roll into
balls about ¾ inch in diameter. Bake on a buttered
cookie sheet, spaced well apart (they'll spread out),
in a preheated 350-degree oven for 15 minutes, or
until lightly golden. Cool on the cookie sheet before
removing.

FIJI STUFFED BANANAS

SERVES 4:

4 large ripe bananas,
peeled and slit down the
center lengthwise; but
do not cut through

1 cup of grated coconut
1 tablespoon of sugar   } blended

4 tablespoons of hot water

Fill the banana slits with the coconut and sugar
mixture, carefully pushing it in with a small spoon.
Arrange the bananas in one layer in a baking dish,
pour the hot water around them, and bake, uncovered,
in a preheated 325-degree oven for 35 minutes. Serve
cold. Ice cream is a good accompaniment.

DEEP-DISH BLUEBERRY PIE

(Alaska)

SERVES 6:

Alaska could be called "The Blueberry State," the tart-sweet berries growing wild everywhere. Alaskans rate cooks by how good their blueberry pies are. They don't "fuss them up," mainly doing as little as possible to change or enhance the personality of the wild berries. They always serve the pie warm accompanied by a lusty scoop of vanilla ice cream. An especially deep pie plate is used, as the berry filling is a thick one.

3 tablespoons of butter	1½ tablespoons of lemon
1½ quarts of blueberries	juice
1 cup of sugar	Pastry for a 1-crust pie
2 tablespoons of flour	(see Rhubarb Pie
	recipe and cut recipe
	in half)

With 1 tablespoon of the butter, butter a deep

9-inch pie plate. In a bowl, gently blend the berries, sugar and flour. Spoon into the pie plate, sprinkle with the lemon juice and dot with the remaining 2 tablespoons butter. Cover with the pastry, flute the edges and cut a vent in the center. Bake in a preheated 425-degree oven for 10 minutes; reduce the heat to 350 degrees and bake for 15 minutes longer or until the crust is golden brown.

BRANDY SNAPS

(New Zealand)

MAKES ABOUT 3 DOZEN SNAPS:

¾ cup of butter
¾ cup of sugar
¾ cup of golden syrup
(light molasses)
¾ cup of sifted all-purpose flour

1½ teaspoons of ground ginger
1½ tablespoons of brandy
Whipped cream flavored with vanilla and sugar

Melt the butter and mix it with the sugar and syrup. In a bowl, blend the flour and ginger, then stir in the butter-sugar-syrup mixture and the brandy, mixing well. Grease a cookie sheet, and, allowing space for the snaps to spread, drop them on the sheet a teaspoonful at a time. Bake in a preheated 325-degree oven for 8 to 10 minutes. Remove and when cool enough to handle, roll each snap on the handle of a wooden spoon, thus ending up with cookie tubes. When cold, using a pastry bag, squeeze the flavored whipped cream into each of the rolled brandy snaps.

CHEESE STRAWS

(New Zealand)

SERVES 4 TO 6:

4 tablespoons of butter
1 cup of flour
¼ teaspoon of salt
    Pinch of cayenne
1 egg, beaten

1 teaspoon of baking
    powder
1 cup of grated sharp
    Cheddar cheese

In a bowl, cut the butter into the flour, then gradually add the remaining ingredients, working into a stiff paste. Lightly flour a pastry board or a piece of waxed paper and roll the dough out into a sheet ⅛ inch thick. With a pastry cutter, cut the dough into long narrow strips resembling straws. Bake on a cookie sheet in a preheated 425-degree oven for 5 minutes, or until golden.

FAIRBANK'S BLUEBERRY FLAPJACKS

(Alaska)

SERVES 6 WITH ABOUT 24 4-INCH-IN-DIAMETER CAKES:

Wild blueberries abound in Alaska and are utilized in many ways, prominent among them these sourdough flapjacks.

5 cups of Sourdough
    Starter (see recipe)
3 cups of warm water
    (not hot!)
3½ cups of flour
3 eggs
3 tablespoons of melted
    butter

½ cup of light cream
1½ teaspoons of baking
    soda
2½ tablespoons of sugar
1½ teaspoons of salt
6 tablespoons of fresh
    blueberries

In a large bowl, mix well the starter, water and flour

until it is smooth. Cover with a towel and set in a warm place for 8 hours. Add the eggs, melted butter and cream, blending until smooth. Stir in the baking soda, sugar and salt.

Cook as you do all pancakes on a hot, greased grill, ladling the batter onto the grill to form cakes of the size you wish. Cook for about 2 minutes, or until tiny bubbles form. Sprinkle a few blueberries on each cake, turn and cook for about 2 minutes.

GRAPEFRUIT ALASKA

SERVES 6:

3 large grapefruit
½ cup plus 2 tablespoons
of sugar
¾ cup of brandy
6 egg whites

¼ teaspoon of salt
1 quart of tart, but creamy
lemon sherbet, frozen
very hard

Halve the grapefruit. Cut out the sections (save the shells to fill later), place them in a bowl and sprinkle with the 2 tablespoons of sugar and brandy. Cover the bowl and refrigerate for 2 hours. Remove the white membrane from the grapefruit shells and refrigerate them 2 hours. In a bowl, beat the egg whites and salt with an electric beater until soft peaks begin to form. Gradually add the ½ cup of sugar and beat until stiff. Place the cold, brandied grapefruit sections in the cold grapefruit shells. Cover with 2 scoops of the sherbet, then cover and seal the tops of the shells with the meringue. Bake in a preheated 450-degree oven until the meringue is lightly golden. Watch carefully. Serve immediately.

KIWI FRUIT

This unique fuzzy Asian fruit, also called Chinese gooseberry, is very popular in New Zealand, and served as a dessert in numerous ways. Just the inner fruit, never the skin, is eaten. Here are some of the ways it is served:

(1) Cut in half and eat as it is with a small spoon.
(2) Slice and serve sprinkled with lemon juice.
(3) Flambé slices with rum.
(4) Offer with cheese, ice cream, yogurt or whipped cream.
(5) Serve atop pies, cakes and tarts.
(6) Arrange slices in an attractive champagne glass and lightly marinate in a good brandy.

New Zealanders are conscious of the fact that a serving of kiwi provides the full daily requirement of vitamin C, and that the fruit contains only 30 calories.

LEMON HONEY

(*New Zealand*)

SERVES 6:

4 lemons	2 cups of sugar
4 eggs, slightly beaten	8 tablespoons of butter

Grate the rind from the lemons being careful not to get any of the white part (zest). Squeeze the juice from the lemons and strain it. Place lemon rind, juice, eggs, sugar and butter into a double boiler. Cook over medium heat, stirring constantly, until the mixture thickens. Do not boil. Cool and serve on pikelets (refer to page 138).

BAKED PAPAYA TAHITI

SERVES 6:

3 small ripe papayas,
  peeled, cut in half
  lengthwise and seeded
¾ cup of sugar

½ cup of water
2 cups of coconut milk
  (see below)

Place the papayas in a baking dish, cut side up, in one layer. Sprinkle with the sugar and pour the water along the sides of the fruit. Basting the fruit every 15 minutes with the sugar-water, bake, uncovered, in a preheated 375-degree oven for 1 hour, or until tender but still firm and intact. When tender, raise the heat to 425 degrees and bake for 3 minutes, or until the liquid becomes caramel-brown. Turn off the oven, fill the papayas with coconut milk and leave in the oven until the milk is warm.

COCONUT MILK

Chop meat from a fresh coconut into small chunks to get 2 cups. Place in a blender, add 2 cups of hot water and blend at high speed for 1½ minutes. Scrape the accumulations from the side of the blender and blend again until the liquid is thick. Over a bowl pour the "milk" into a strainer lined with 2 thicknesses of damp cheesecloth. With a wooden spoon or pestle, press the blended coconut hard against the strainer, extracting as much of the liquid as possible. Then bring the ends of the cheesecloth together and wring it out into the bowl. Discard the pulp left in the cheesecloth. One cup of chopped coconut and 1 cup of water produce 1 cup of coconut milk.

FIJI PAPAYA CUSTARD

SERVES 6:

2 tablespoons of butter
1½ cups of shredded,
lightly toasted fresh
coconut
3 cups of peeled, diced
ripe papaya, mashed
into a pulp
6 eggs, beaten
¼ teaspoon of salt

¼ cup of sugar
1 quart of medium
cream, scalded (not
too hot or it will
curdle the eggs)
1 teaspoon of vanilla
Grated rind, juice and
minced pulp of
1 orange

Butter a baking dish with the butter. Evenly spread
the coconut, then the papaya on the bottom of the
dish. In a bowl, blend the eggs, salt and sugar and
beating constantly, gradually pour in the hot cream.
Skim off any bubbles from the top. Stir to make certain
the sugar is dissolved, then blend in the vanilla and
orange rind, juice and pulp. Stir well and spoon over
the coconut and papaya in the baking dish. Place
the dish in a pan with 1 inch of hot water, and bake,
uncovered, in a preheated 350-degree oven for 40
minutes, or until set and the inserted blade of a knife
comes out clean. Cool, then chill. Loosen with the
blade of a knife run gently around the edges and
invert on a serving platter, the coconut and papaya on
top.

PIKELETS

(New Zealand)

SERVES 8:

2 eggs
2 tablespoons of sugar
1 tablespoon of melted
butter
1 cup of milk

2 cups of flour
1 teaspoon of baking soda
1 "heaping" teaspoon of
cream of tartar

In a bowl, beat the eggs until light, then beat in the sugar. Blend the melted butter and the milk. Gradually blend in the flour, baking soda and cream of tartar. Beat together into a creamy consistency. Cook the little pancakes on a very hot, well-greased griddle, dropping the batter on a tablespoonful at a time. When bubbling, turn the pikelets, cooking until light brown. Serve immediately with Lemon Honey.

TAHITIAN PINEAPPLE SNOW

SERVES 8:

3½ cups of pineapple juice
3 envelopes of unflavored gelatin
6 tablespoons of sugar
¼ teaspoon of salt
1 tablespoon of grated lemon rind
4 tablespoons of fresh lemon juice

1½ cups of heavy cream, whipped
1½ cups of grated coconut
4 cups of fresh strawberries, cut into halves
4 pineapple slices, quartered

In a bowl, blend 1 cup of the pineapple juice with the gelatin and sugar; let set for 5 minutes. Place the bowl over a pan containing 2 cups of boiling water, stirring until the gelatin is dissolved. In a bowl, blend the remaining 2½ cups of pineapple juice, salt, lemon rind and lemon juice. Stir in the gelatin mixture and refrigerate until it has the consistency of unbeaten egg whites. Beat it until fluffy; fold in the whipped cream and ¾ cup of the coconut. Spoon into a 2-quart mold and refrigerate until firmly set. Unmold on a serving dish. Sprinkle with coconut, top with strawberries and surround with the pineapple, the remaining strawberries and coconut.

PAVLOVA

(Australia and New Zealand)

SERVES 4 TO 6:

4 egg whites	1 circular piece of wax
Pinch of salt	paper, 8 inches in
1 cup of fine sugar	diameter, buttered with
1 teaspoon of white	1 tablespoon of butter
vinegar	1 cup of whipping cream,
1 teaspoon of vanilla	whipped
	Sliced fruit

Beat the egg whites with the salt until they are stiff and dry; gradually beat in the sugar, then the vinegar and vanilla. Hold the piece of wax paper under very cold water, then place it on a cold cookie sheet. Spoon the mixture evenly onto the wax paper and cook in a preheated 250-degree oven for 1½ hours. Turn the oven off and leave the pavlova in for 30 minutes to cool gradually, so the shell won't crack. Remove the wax paper carefully and serve crowned with the whipped cream and decorated with sliced fruit such as kiwi, peaches, passion fruit or strawberries.

POE

(*Tahitian Baked Fruit*)

SERVES 12 TO 14:

2 medium-sized ripe papayas, peeled, seeded and cut into chunks

2 small very ripe pineapples, peeled, quartered, cored and cut into chunks

2 medium-sized ripe mangoes, peeled, seeded and cut into chunks

2 pounds of ripe bananas, peeled and cut into chunks

½ cup of arrowroot

1 cup of dark brown sugar

1½ teaspoons of vanilla

3 tablespoons of softened butter

Chop the fruit in a meat chopper, using the coarse blade. Place in a strainer over a bowl, stirring until all the liquid has drained. In another bowl, combine 1 cup of the liquid and the arrowroot. Take the fruit out of the strainer and stir it into the bowl with the arrowroot mixture, then slowly stir in the remaining fruit liquid, the brown sugar and the vanilla. With the soft butter, evenly grease a large, shallow baking dish. Spread the fruit evenly in the dish. Bake, uncovered, in a preheated 375-degree oven for 1 hour, or until top is golden brown. Cool, then cover and refrigerate for 5 hours.

RHUBARB PIE

(Alaska)

SERVES 6:

Alaska is noted for its rhubarb, which can grow as high as four feet, and especially for its famous variety, Red Chipman. Thus, with such a crop available nearly everywhere, rhubarb, in one form or another, rates high on the list of desserts.

PASTRY FOR TWO-CRUST PIE

2 cups of flour   ⅓ cup of shortening
1 teaspoon of salt   ⅓ cup of ice water
⅛ cup of butter

In a bowl, sift the flour and salt and cut in the butter and Crisco with a pastry cutter until the mixture has the consistency of cornmeal. Mix in the water with a fork, and then work with your hands until the dough can be easily shaped into a ball. Wrap in wax paper and refrigerate for 1½ hours. Cut the ball in half and on a lightly floured board roll each half into a sheet about ⅛ inch thick. With one sheet, line the sides and bottom of a 9-inch pie plate. Refrigerate while preparing the filling.

FILLING

3 cups of rhubarb, cut
into ½-inch slices
1½ tablespoons of lemon
juice
2 tablespoons of flour

1½ cups of sugar
2 egg yolks, beaten
slightly
⅛ teaspoon of salt

Take the pie plate and dough from the refrigerator
and line the bottom of the plate with the rhubarb
slices. In a bowl, blend lemon juice, flour, sugar, egg
yolks and salt and spoon it evenly over the rhubarb.
Cover with the second sheet of pastry. Flute the
edges and with a knife slash the top crust in several
places. Cook in a preheated 400-degree oven for 20
minutes. Lower heat to 350 degrees and cook an addi-
tional 15 minutes, or until the crust is golden brown.

SOURDOUGH STARTER
(Alaska)

MAKES ABOUT 6 CUPS, ENOUGH FOR 12 SMALL LOAVES:

*Sourdough starter may take several tries before
success. It all depends upon the right mixture of flour
and yeast and proper fermentation. If you like the
flavor, but not the fuss, many bakeries sell the sourdough starter. But it's worth the little effort to try to
make it, the flavor is unique.*

6 cups of flour
2 packages of active dry
yeast

5 cups of warm water
(not hot!)

Place the flour in a large bowl, form a well in the
center and gradually add the yeast and water. Slowly
blend the flour, yeast and water until well mixed, then
beat well with an electric beater until the dough is very
smooth. Cover the bowl (with a cloth, as a little air
should enter), place in a warm place without drafts
and leave for 24 hours. By this time the mixture
should have started to ferment, bubble; if it hasn't

you must forget this batch and start all over again. When you have taken the amount of starter you want for baking, place the rest in a glass jar with a screw-top, so it can be tightly sealed. Refrigerate. The starter keeps for over a month.

ALASKAN SOURDOUGH BREAD

MAKE 6 LOAVES:

2 cups of Sourdough Starter (see preceding recipe)
13 to 14 cups of flour
4 cups of warm water (not hot!)
6 tablespoons of vegetable oil

2 teaspoons of salt
1 teaspoon of baking soda
6 tablespoons of sugar
5 tablespoons of soft butter

In a large bowl, place the starter, 5 cups of flour and the warm water, blending well until the mixture is smooth. Cover with a cloth and place in a warm, draftless place for 8 hours. Blend in 8 cups of the flour, oil, salt, baking soda and sugar, mixing it until the flour is completely absorbed and the dough can be formed into a ball. If it is too soft to shape easily into a ball, work in the remaining flour, a little at a time, until the dough is of the right consistency to handle. On a floured pastry board, work the dough, kneading it and pressing it with your hands, until you have it smooth and elastic. Roll it into a ball and place it into a bowl, covered with a cloth, and set in a warm place for 4 hours, or until it has doubled in bulk. Butter the sides and bottom of six 9 x 5 x 3-inch loaf pans. Cut the ball of dough into 6 equal parts. Pat each into a loaf with your hands and place in the pans. Let set, uncovered, in a warm place for 1½ hours, so the loaves rise to about twice original size. Bake in a preheated 375-degree oven for about 1½ hours, or until the loaves are brown, but not crusty-brown.

INDEX